This book is a gift

From:

To:

Enjoy and Share

FORGET
HAPPINESS

Seven Steps to a Fulfilled Life

MICHAEL KOULY

First Edition

**Book 4 of the
Self-leadership Book Series**

ISBN
978-0-9992181-6-7

To my father, Mgr. Paul Kouly, for being a remarkable example of a purpose-driven and fulfilling life, and in loving memory of my mother, Helen Kouly, for her selfless life of love, dedication, and sacrifice.

Thank you!

You were born with potential.
You were born with goodness and trust.
You were born with ideals and dreams.
You were born with greatness.
You were born with wings.
You are not meant for crawling, so don't.
You have wings.
Learn to use them and fly.

– Rumi

CONTENTS

Acknowledgements   9

Why This Book   10

Introduction   24

1. Emptiness   40

2. Courage   65

3. Self-discovery: Defining Your Purpose   87

4. Transformation: Pursuing your Purpose   127

5. Love   160

6. Living In Line With Your Purpose   190

7. Fulfillment   207

Notes   226

About The Author   237

ACKNOWLEDGMENTS

I would like to acknowledge the invaluable contributions of the following good people: Marwa Itani, I thank you for beautifully translating my thoughts into the elegant chapters in this book. Thank you, Mary Shammas, Susan Simmons, Dr. Susan Murray, Dr. Wafa Skaff, Hala Mourady, and Roy Sayegh for your feedback on the content. Thank you, Mary Shammas for designing the creative cover and illustrations, and for formatting the book for publishing. Furthermore, I would like to thank Roy Sayegh for proofreading, and Jo Lavender for impeccable editing and instrumental recommendations.

Last, but not least: special thanks go out to you, dear reader, for having the courage and strength to embark on the journey of fulfillment. We all deserve to live a fulfilled life, and we are all capable of seeing that right realized.

WHY THIS BOOK

The moment the door opened and I walked into the house, I could smell the musky odor and see the haze of smoke drifting out of the adjacent room. Inside the room, I found a group of people sitting, relaxing, and smoking marijuana. This was the scent and scene that greeted me when I recently visited some acquaintances. When cannabis was legalized for recreational use, the couple, along with their two adult children, and in this case their children's friends from university, made this a weekend ritual. The couple were hard-working professionals, and after a long week of work, they would find some time to indulge in this practice to unwind and de-stress.

This story may seem strange to some, but I don't mention it to pass judgment on my acquaintances' weekend rituals. Instead, I want to take this incident as an example of the trends I have been observing and reading about for some time. I would like to take a risk and make a few predictions about our twenty-first century:

- In many parts of the world, such weekend rituals will become more common.

- The use of cannabis will become almost universally accepted and legalized. It may still be prohibited in some countries, of course, for religious and cultural reasons.

- Some tobacco companies will move into the cannabis industry, as its success will parallel their existing business.

- More governments will opt for legalizing and taxing the cannabis industry as a solution to some social and legal drug-related problems, as well as a good source of government income.

- In the long term, more potent forms of synthetic drugs will be created and spread, as conventional cannabis will fall short of delivering the required sensation.

- Eventually some of these strong synthetic substances will also become legalized and taxable, following the same path as cannabis to become socially and legally accepted.

We are also facing higher levels of mental illnesses, specifically anxiety disorders, depression, and other mood-related disorders. Research from the National Center for Health Statistics shows that the reported rates of depression have increased significantly, and the use of anti-depressants by individuals aged 12 and above has increased 400% from 1988-1994 to 2005-2008[1]. Therefore, I predict that:

- Depression and other mental disorders will reach significantly higher levels, affecting a greater percentage of the world's population.

- The number of people on antidepressants and anti-anxiety medications will continue to increase.

Finally, we are witnessing an unprecedented rate of change and advancement in technology, and I believe that:

- The twenty-first and twenty-second centuries will be the most exciting centuries in the last few millennia in terms of technological advancements and scientific breakthroughs[2], which may lead to solutions to major social challenges, and cures for physiological illnesses.

- The twenty-first century will be called "the age of artificial intelligence and robotics." It will also be known as "the century of mental health illnesses" and possibly "spiritual emptiness."

I am not sure if all the above predictions will come true, but what I am sure of is that we are living in a world that is moving too fast for us. Life is becoming more complicated, and we are facing increasing pressure to cope with the unnatural pace of change.

Author Alberto Villoldo wrote that we originally evolved to deal with one lion roaring at us at a time, triggering an occasional stressful fight-or-flight response. Although such an incident was intense, it was rare, and recurring intense stress was therefore an unusual experience.

These days, Villoldo said, we have created a totally different world, with our almost constant media exposure to terrible occurrences across the globe. We are not built to withstand this kind of intensity, fear, and anxiety, especially over a prolonged period. It is like living in a jungle with fierce beasts threatening us at all times; we are not able to relax and calm down, because there is constant pressure to survive[3].

Although we are designed to adapt and evolve, explosive change and constant stimulation have become a part of our lives too quickly for us to adjust to them, and this is putting pressure on us to find new ways to cope. The amount of information we are bombarded with in one month, via conventional and social media, exceeds the amount of information most people processed in an entire lifetime a few centuries ago[4].

This pressure is getting worse. Social media and advanced marketing practices are making it harder for us to adapt to this over-stimulation. They are intentionally utilizing psychological tricks to prey on our fears and emotional needs, to get us hooked on our smartphones and their applications, and to drive us to consume.

It has reached a point where social media addictions are common. There have been several alarming studies done on how many times people check their smartphones every day[5]. This is added to the anxiety that many people feel about maximizing the views and "likes" on their social media posts[6].

If the rate of change on the outside exceeds the rate of change on the inside, the end is near.

– Jack Welch

In such an environment, we find ourselves constantly in physical, mental, social, and emotional survival mode. We are distracted and do not have enough time, space, and silence to reflect on core issues that would fulfill us, like meaning, purpose, and building deep, genuine, and constructive relationships.

We are stuck in the rapids, tumbling and being swept down the river, fighting to stay afloat and draw breath. It can be so overwhelming and tiring that many of us cannot muster up the strength to swim against the current.

This is an urgent matter that we all need to address, for our own sakes, for the sakes of our loved ones, and for the sakes of those around us. This is something that exists in our current reality, and it will become worse as time goes on.

Life is moving too fast, and we need to focus on the core issues before we find ourselves too far down the river. If we don't concentrate on meaning, purpose, and responsibility to help anchor our lives, we allow an emptiness to form inside us. The longer we get caught up in shallowness and temporary distractions, the more we have to exist in survival mode, and the more the emptiness will grow.

A Walk Through History

Before The Nineteenth Century

People before the nineteenth century experienced a predominantly stable rate of change; it happened at such a slow pace that, apart from rare breakthroughs, it took years for the change to have much impact. In general, people lived simply, mostly congregated in villages or towns, and their paths in life were almost set from the day they were born.

People were mainly focused on manual jobs, such as farming, carpentry, and stonemasonry; their children usually followed in their footsteps (a farmer's children often became farmers). It was uncommon for people to move across social classes or into radically different professions.

Many people also had strong relationships with family members, neighbors, and the community. Religious institutions held sway over the people and promoted moral values like contentment, patience, and simplicity. All in all, this relatively low-stress atmosphere ensured individuals could find support during difficult times. Most people did not abuse substances, and, although the lack of diagnoses available at the time makes it difficult to be sure, it seems that depression and anxiety disorders were not as prevalent as they are today.

The Nineteenth Century

The Industrial Age set a faster pace. Factories were built in cities, mass production became the norm, and the need for an industrial labor force encouraged people from nearby villages and towns to migrate to the cities.

The population density increased rapidly as more people relocated. Many neighborhoods became so crowded that people were living in terrible, unsanitary conditions, crammed into unsuitable housing and often sharing one room between an entire family[7].

Life became more complicated. Change was happening on many different fronts. People had to work longer hours, learn new trades, or learn how to operate machinery so they could get a job. They had to exchange the comfort of fields and open spaces for small lodgings and cramped, polluted neighborhoods. The stress and pressure of this new lifestyle required different ways of dealing with the change and with one another. People's relationships changed and became more stressful, and the support they had relied on in the past declined.

Education became publicly accessible and more mainstream[8]; children were expected to go to school so that they could enter new professions (e.g. technicians, engineers, lawyers) that were demanded by the new industrial economy and the societal changes it caused[9]. Homework helped to increase the rate of learning, and some less fortunate families could not keep their children in school. These children would join the workforce early and be exposed to additional work-related stress earlier in their lives – child labor was a common practice[10].

The old ways of coping with the pressure of change and stress no longer worked. People needed something stronger than praying, being part of nature, and being part of a community, so they resorted to increased consumption of alcohol and, in some cases, stronger drugs.

The Twentieth Century

Technological breakthroughs and advanced production techniques added more pressure to the existing issues of the nineteenth century. Cities again increased in size and population, and the stress of keeping up with the boost in technology, as well as the competition over jobs and resources, made life more complicated.

Furthermore, the twentieth century witnessed the introduction and spread of processed foods, plastics, home appliances, and affordable automobiles, which became a necessity in many households, particularly in the Western Hemisphere. Aggressive marketing and mass advertising turned most communities into consumer societies, struggling to keep up with the demands of the modern lifestyle. While science added years to the average human lifespan, the new way of living led to a wider spread of cancer and cardiovascular and stress-related illnesses.

Added to this, humanity also suffered through two world wars, nuclear threats, and an unprecedented level of media exposure to global violence.

This exposure was partly down to the introduction of commercial computers, the internet, and mobile phones. We became more globally connected, had more access to information, and witnessed unprecedented technological growth.

Life became more complicated, stress levels soared, and people were unable to cope. Instead of focusing on finding meaning, purpose, and spiritual growth, people's lives became centered around materialism and the pursuit of financial and social success (as defined by the corporate world and the values of consumer societies).

Stress increased to such high levels that new concepts – like stress and anger management – were created to help people. However, for many who could not "manage" their stress in functional and healthy ways, maladaptive coping mechanisms were the solution.

Television became the default distraction for the majority of people. Religious morals and family values took a back seat when it came to providing comfort and stress relief, while substance abuse and addictions to heavy drugs dramatically increased.

Today: The Twenty-First Century

Many people recognize that we live in highly stressful environments. Life is complicated and sometimes overwhelming. We are still in the first quarter of the twenty-first century, and we are already witnessing technologies that seem straight out of a science fiction novel.

The fast pace that these new technologies have set has led many of us to desire instant gratification. The available services reflect this: think about Amazon and imagine future home deliveries by drones.

To summarize, some of the issues we are facing include:

- Relationships have become shallower; people are not learning how to build strong and meaningful connections.

- Family values are weaker and hold less sway over us.

- Materialism and consumerism are increasing.

- Excessive individualism and personal success have become more important. Competitiveness is now a desired and encouraged attitude; everyone wants the best for themselves, even if others pay the price for their actions.

- People constantly want more, and they want it instantly, without reciprocating with effort.

- Support structures (like family, religious institutions, strong communal ties) have weakened, so we are missing a crucial, scientifically-proven way to cope with stress.

- The global population is rapidly expanding, increasing the pressure on natural resources and heightening the sense of competition and excessive individualism.

We don't feel that we have enough time to deal with stress, so we want quick fixes. We want to feel happy now, but we are unwilling to put in the effort to achieve true happiness. Instead, we unknowingly pursue the shallow and temporary feeling of "happiness," which is more like constant positive stimulation than deep internal joy and contentment.

We are entering the age of Artificial Intelligence (AI). Although it will make our lives easier in many ways, some of the greatest minds of our time, like the late Stephen

Hawking, have said AI could pose a major threat to the existence of the entire human species[11].

We are already seeing reports that almost 50% of jobs will become obsolete in the next two decades or so, thanks to robotics and AI[12]. Even our education system, still working on the industrial revolution model, is unable to keep up with the social, technological, and economic changes. As I am writing checks to my children's school, I am reading articles about how the expensive education they are currently getting will become obsolete by the time my youngest graduates from college. You can imagine the pressures they will face as they grow.

Consider what life will be like for the future human population (projected to be nearly 10 billion by 2050[13]). They are expected to find work opportunities, establish homes, pursue comfortable lives, be rich, sexy, cool, and famous, all while trying to deal with the major reductions in jobs and the mounting competition over resources. How will they be able to cope with such a life?

The upcoming challenges will dwarf those of the twentieth century. It is therefore time that we teach ourselves and our loved ones how to focus on something deeper, more profound, and more controllable than living by the norms of the outside world.

Unfortunately, many of us would rather look for distractions than take the time to understand the nature of our current reality, and to realize who we are and what we are capable of overcoming. If we don't learn to address the feeling of emptiness that results from not living a full life, we might resort to escape mechanisms or maladaptive coping strategies such as:

- Alcohol and tobacco.

- Illicit drugs.

- Excessive video gaming.

- Excessive television and movies (where you immerse yourself in a fake reality as an escape).

- Excessive internet browsing without purpose.

- Excessive social media use.

Feeling depressed and overwhelmed already? Stay with me, good news is on the way!

The Good News

It is not all doom and gloom. People have started noticing and addressing these negative trends, and the value of searching for meaning and purpose is becoming recognized, by both organizations and individuals. Joy, peace of mind, and purpose are being prioritized, and this is transforming lives for the better. However, it is also causing its own problems.

As a response to their awareness of the negativity, many people are actively trying to find "happiness." There has been a surge of books and workshops centered around this subject. Unfortunately, the word has become abused and commercialized. Happiness is often defined in shallow ways and, as a result, true happiness has become elusive and made the problem of emptiness worse.

People are lost because they have made the decision to deal with the emptiness and pursue happiness, but they have found a shallow kind of happiness, like a mirage, and the best it has to offer is some momentary relief. It is not enough to sustain us from day to day. We need to forget about looking for surface and fleeting happiness.

We need to stop limiting ourselves and focus on digging deeper to get to the true happiness we all deserve. True happiness can only be experienced through fulfillment.

This book was written to help you on your own journey of finding fulfillment. It is time for you to achieve what is most important: living a purposeful life and sharing it with others. Allow yourself to seek meaning and embrace a state of fulfillment so that you may live deeply, profoundly, and happily.

True happiness is the by-product of a fulfilled life.

Welcome to Fulfillment...

INTRODUCTION

> **There's nothing you can do that's more important than being fulfilled. You become a sign, you become a signal, transparent to transcendence; in this way, you will find, live, and become a realization of your own personal myth.**

– Joseph Campbell

Humans are special. Our potential bubbles just beneath the surface of our beings. We need to tap into this source, appreciate its power, and utilize its strength. We all deserve to live fulfilled lives, but sometimes past events, wounds, obligations, or distractions can stand in the way. The pressure to conform to our constantly changing environments makes it difficult for us to live the lives we deserve.

Realizing our potential isn't easy; nothing truly beautiful in life ever is. It requires time and effort, belief, work, discipline, commitment, and the willpower to overcome obstacles. Is it worth these things? I like to think so. After all, what is the alternative? Living a mediocre, pale, empty, and miserable life? This book is meant to help you find yourself and reflect on how you can bring meaning and fulfillment to your life and make the story of your personal journey worth telling.

First things first: **there is no such thing as happiness,** or at least, not the happiness most people talk about. The idea of "happiness" seems to follow us everywhere. Consider how we prioritize it when making a decision or thinking about the future. Examples of this might be: "I just want you to be happy," "eat it, if it will make you happy," "buy it, if it makes you happy," or "who can put a price on happiness?"

For many, happiness is the notion that we should strive to live a life filled with "happy feelings." This suggests that if you are not constantly, or at least predominantly, feeling happy, there is something wrong with you. This sets impossible and unhealthy standards, and creates frustration and dissatisfaction.

It's important to feel the full spectrum of emotions. You need to be able to handle twists and turns, and experience emotions without letting them overwhelm you. Think of emotions like colors; you need more than one to paint a beautiful picture. You need dark colors and light colors to give depth and energy to a canvas. Life is full of experiences, good and bad, and these are what make life rich. Even (or especially) moments that challenge us help us learn and grow.

Happiness is an emotional state. Emotions fluctuate. They are reactions to your thoughts at a specific time and place. Your mind will interpret your surroundings, and, based on those interpretations, you will experience temporary emotions. This transient nature is one reason why you should not make happiness, or any other temporary and unstable emotion, your ultimate purpose.

Many of us will create scenarios about what perfect happiness looks like, and how we can achieve it. Although moments of happiness (e.g. succeeding in an endeavor, buying a new house, traveling) will be briefly satisfying, most people will feel a lingering sense of "something is missing." These happy moments will pass as soon as the hype surrounding them fades. They feel briefly great, but in a few days or weeks, the initial excitement will plateau.

Happiness is changeable and subject to outside forces – it is temporary. There is something much deeper, more durable, and more substantial that you need to attain in order to experience a purposeful and meaningful life, which does not depend on outside influences. This is fulfillment.

Instead of aiming for fleeting happiness, find something that lasts longer. Derive meaning from the actions that you take and the people in your life. As humans, one of our greatest needs is connections.

Life is about connections, because we know that we cannot survive alone – and we also can never really be alone. We must recognize that we are standing alongside many others, possibly living under the same roof, and that our fates are intertwined. If you poke a hole in a boat, one side might fill up faster, but eventually the entire boat will go down. We can either choose to ignore the hole and hope it will get better on its own, or we can help to fix it.

We need to truly grasp the fundamental truth that the more we serve and help others, the more people become elevated, and the more we ourselves become elevated. As social beings, we have always survived better in groups, and if the group benefits, the individual does too.

When you contribute to the survival and growth of the whole by offering them the best version of yourself, this leads to a far more intense feeling than happiness. It provides meaning, allowing you to transcend yourself and live purposefully. Your actions are no longer focused upon your own well-being, but upon something which will outlast you. This means that the feeling has far more permanence.

Joy, rather than happiness, is the goal of life, for joy is the emotion which accompanies our fulfilling our natures as human beings. It is based on the experience of one's identity as a being of worth and dignity.

– *Rollo May*

Let's take a closer look at the word "fulfillment." At its core, it comes from the word "full." You are fulfilled when you lead a full life – but what does a full life mean?

When we see a glass on the table with no liquid inside, we classify the glass as empty. However, in reality, it is not empty. It is filled with air. When we refer to something as empty, it means that it is not filled with anything of substance. Individuals can have lives that are filled with many distractions and activities, but they are not necessarily full, because the distractions and activities are not providing them with real substance.

Fulfillment is a more intense and stable feeling than happiness. It is more a state of being than an emotion. It carries many positive emotions with it, but also envelopes the negative ones and gives them meaning as part of the overall structure of life, which helps you through them, rather than letting them weigh you down. Fulfillment allows you to experience the full spectrum of emotions, and puts the negative ones into a picture where they have beauty and significance, rather than existing as sources of stress with no picture to contextualize them.

It is a long road to reach fulfillment, but it is key to truly experiencing a "full" life. Unfortunately, many of us struggle with just the first steps. It is important to become aware of your own actions and your coping methods, your favorite ways of trying to escape and hide, because once you are able to unlock your potential, you will be surprised by your strength.

A man was once told that he had one month to live. Before that specific moment, he had lived an average life. He had a routine and did all the things that most people thought made them "happy." He had a nice house, a nice car, and a lovely family, but his career took most of his attention, and he did not have time to appreciate those around him.

When he found out that he had one month to live, everything changed. Every minute became valuable. He started to focus on love: love of everything. He spent more time with his family in that month than he had in the previous year. He wanted to make sure that all his interactions had meaning and purpose. One of the first things he did was to forgive others for past mistakes and to forgive himself as well. He started to see his problems in a new way. They were smaller than they used to seem, and the concerns that had filled up most of his days became almost irrelevant.

Suddenly, it all seemed light. He wanted to savor every moment. He tried foods he had previously been unwilling to try, and he participated in activities which he had been afraid to attempt. He was finally seeing the world clearly. The emptiness he had once felt was now filled with love and appreciation, which he gave back to others in buckets. He wanted people to relish life as he did in that very moment, as he was approaching death – he had realized his purpose. He lived more in that one month than he had in the rest of his life.

Faced with death, he found a way to make his life meaningful and enjoyable for himself and those around him. However, this does not mean you have to wait until you are dealing with such news to change your perspective on your own life.

Positive perceptions and the feeling of fulfillment, purpose, and meaning are all linked to a longer life span. This notion is supported by a study about aging published in the Lancet, conducted by researchers in University College London, Princeton University, and Stony Brook University. The research showed that those with the highest eudaimonic well-being[1] were 30% less likely to die over the 8½ year study[2]. When you focus on meaning, less things in your life will be stressful, and you can impact more people with your conscious and focused actions.

The above study may have illustrated the importance of living a fulfilled life, but how do you get there? What does the journey look like? What are the steps that you need to take?

After years of careful and extensive observation of thousands of people who went through the intensive and transformational leadership programs that I conduct around the world, I have developed the model of fulfillment that I believe acknowledges our actual reality and the full potential of human nature.

The following model was established to give you a clearer picture of the road ahead. In this book, I shall compare finding fulfillment to a journey where you go through the process of scoping out your options, picking a destination, booking a ticket, and taking off.

Of course, no journey is ever entirely smooth; you will have delays, diversions, lost baggage, and overall turbulence throughout. Despite all this, the journey will be filled with beautiful moments of growth, and in the end, you will come out much stronger because of it.

This model/journey provides you with the tools of awareness that you will need to spot the warning signs and not slip back into old ways of thinking. I find that when we break things down into steps, they sometimes feel less daunting. The journey is long and difficult, but we can all "walk" it; it just takes the right amount of awareness and a deep level of appreciation for your life, which deserves to be lived to the fullest.

> When the suffering becomes acute enough, one goes forward.
>
> *– Hermann Hesse*

Take some time to consider a few questions about your own perception of happiness: what do your moments of happiness look like? What feelings do you experience? Do they represent true and deep happiness?

THE ROADMAP
TO FULFILLMENT

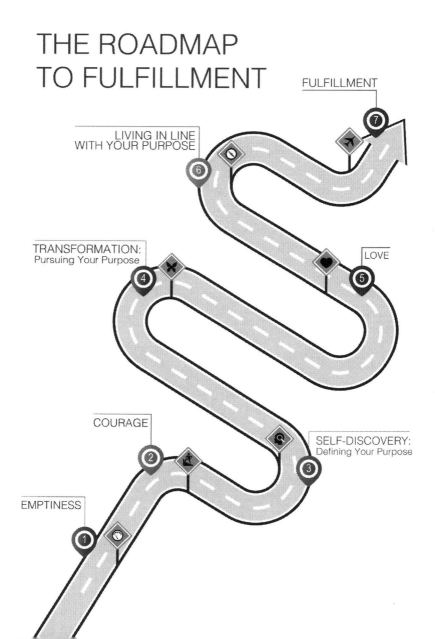

FULFILLMENT

LIVING IN LINE
WITH YOUR PURPOSE

TRANSFORMATION:
Pursuing Your Purpose

LOVE

COURAGE

SELF-DISCOVERY:
Defining Your Purpose

EMPTINESS

The Fulfillment Journey

We'll now consider the 7 steps to fulfillment in brief summaries; these will then be expanded upon throughout the rest of the book, with a chapter dedicated to each step.

Step 1: Emptiness

None of us will try to seek fulfillment if we do not feel as though there is something missing. When we are born, we are usually blissfully unaware of the burden that we may soon have to carry. As we grow older and realize that the world does not in fact revolve around us, our fulfillment levels begin to decrease, until we are adults and weighed down by hardships, challenges, responsibilities, pain, and bills. We may start to approach our days with a mentality of survival, without realizing that the fulfillment we felt as children is buried under the car payments.

Many people will start to spiral downwards and mask this dissatisfaction with distractions, essentially sticking a Band-Aid over the feeling. When we experience negative emotions, stress, or the sense that "something is missing," many of us start saying "I just want to be happy." It is during trying times that we feel the deep pain of emptiness more keenly, and it's crucial that we are aware of the feeling so that we can find ways to address it, instead of letting it perpetually exist in the background.

Not many people will get a red flag like the man who had a month left to live. Most people will live their lives exactly the way they think they "should," as dictated by society, and then realize that they have grown old without ever feeling true satisfaction. Acknowledging and profoundly experiencing the emptiness serves as your red flag, hopefully motivating you to book a ticket to your new destination.

Step 2: Courage

When you recognize the emptiness, the first question that you might ask yourself is: how can I get rid of it? You will have to start looking inward and discovering yourself more deeply, which takes courage.

Courage helps you recognize that there is something much more important than fear. It helps you overcome the overwhelming feelings of emptiness so that you can unlock your true potential.

The decision to change does not come easily and you will experience some internal and external resistance. You will need to summon up your inner strength and resolve so that you can face the pain of emptiness, embrace it, and motivate yourself to strive toward change. With courage, you can uphold your decisions despite your fears. In our travel analogy, courage is deciding to go online and scope out your options.

The drivers of courage at this stage might be the unbearable pain of emptiness, the sweet feeling of self-worth, or the combination of both.

Step 3: Self-Discovery: Purpose

As with other problems, you need to study the situation and try to discover the root of the issue. That is why one of the essential steps of the model is looking inward. Discover who you truly are as a person and think about what you want in life. In our journey analogy, this is the stage where you start to narrow down your options and decide which one best matches your needs and wants.

Self-discovery includes understanding your own thoughts, emotions, and actions, realizing what motivates you, identifying what gives you meaning, discovering what makes you unique, and unveiling what you feel you have to offer to the world. This will help you work out what you should focus on. It is about finding your goodness, beauty, and worthiness despite the obstacles you face.

Step 4: Transformation

Once you are aware of what is standing in your way, it is time to try and deal with it. At this point, you have bought the ticket and you are actually undertaking the first part of the journey (catching a ride to the airport, checking in, security check). Are you ready for take-off, though?

The transformation step (in my opinion) is the hardest. You will have to utilize your courage and your sense of purpose to progress. You must be willing to make the necessary changes and adopt all the qualities of your most authentic and beautiful self. This takes time, effort, resolve, and courage. Transformation will only begin once you realize your self-worth, experience self-love, and feel excited and enthusiastic about who you could become.

This is the most difficult step because it involves revolutionizing your habits and the way you lead your life. It is about learning to accept, forgive, and move beyond your mistakes so you can appreciate yourself and keep journeying forward.

Resistance will constantly be present, and you will hear the siren song of your comfort zone coaxing you not to board the plane, and to return to the safety of home. Push ahead! Every step closer to fulfillment is worth the effort it takes.

Step 5: Love

Healthy self-love is not narcissistic or selfish. It is also not a justification of our weaknesses and the dark side of human nature; it doesn't forget these things, but exists in spite of them.

Healthy self-love is necessary to ensure that you want the best for yourself and your group, without infringing on the rights of others, or abandoning your responsibilities to them. Love is a force that keeps you moving forward, drives you to be courageous, to look within, to transform, and to stick to the journey.

Love in our travel analogy is the inner voice that motivates you to click that mouse, choose your destination, book your ticket, go through security, and board the plane. It's also the fuel of the plane, giving it the ability to fly. Giving and receiving love is essential for creating connections, which ultimately give you meaning and keep you on the path of improvement.

Love goes hand-in-hand with courage, self-discovery, and transformation as you move forward in your journey towards fulfillment. Each step you take brings you closer to seeing and accepting who you are. This increases the likelihood of living in line with your authentic self.

Self-love is about appreciating the goodness within you. It is about appreciating your capacity to serve and love others. It is about appreciating your ability to grow, develop, mature, and continuously improve the reality you and others face.

Healthy self-love is also about appreciating your strengths, resilience, wisdom, and your ability to do the right thing and make smart and virtuous decisions. In essence, it is about your belief that you deserve to live in a better reality, and that you can create this reality for yourself, while helping others do the same in their lives.

Healthy self-love fills you up and allows you to pass it on to others. Love is the glue that holds the entire model, especially the transformational changes, together, discouraging you from slipping back into your old dysfunctional habits. At this point, you truly believe that you deserve better – that you deserve fulfillment.

Step 6: Living In Line With Your Purpose

Only once you appreciate yourself and your life can

you start to live the way that you were meant to. You have boarded the plane, and taken off. Living purposefully and meaningfully means becoming the best that you can be and sharing yourself with the world. In return, people will be inspired by your commitment to what gives you meaning and fulfillment.

It does not mean that you are always "happy," but the meaning that you extract from being authentic to yourself will provide a sense of inner peace, a calmness within the storm that is life. It is the only way to experience life with full intensity. The alternative is living a life that is but a fraction of the one you were meant to live.

Living in line with your purpose can be a liberating experience because you will respect and appreciate yourself enough to embody your true potential and elevate others along the way. It provides you with meaning, which will quell the emptiness and leave you fulfilled.

Step 7: Fulfillment

Finally… fulfillment. This is not about material gain, professional success, or obtaining approval from others. It is not about being rich and famous. It is a state of being where you experience the peace and serenity that come from authenticity; that come from walking your own unique path, which has been carved by you and you alone. Cruising at 35,000 feet, you look out of the window and you realize you are finally on the journey that you have chosen; it is about the appreciation of that moment.

Fulfillment comes with the understanding that you are aligned with your purpose and that every action you take, large or small, is working toward this purpose and giving your life its deepest meaning. Once you have confronted your inner demons, found enough courage and love to take the necessary steps toward change, and you are finally living the truest version of yourself, you will find meaning, inner peace, beauty, fullness, and joy.

Joy breeds more joy; similarly love breeds more love. When you are fulfilled and sharing your fulfillment with others, you pass your elevation on to them. The meaning that this brings is indescribable.

This model is a process, and it is not an easy one to follow. It may take a long time to complete, but once you have reached the end (fulfillment and the inner peace that comes with it), you will realize that the journey was worth every second, and that it was inevitable in order to liberate yourself from the pain of living a shallow, superficial, meaningless and empty life.

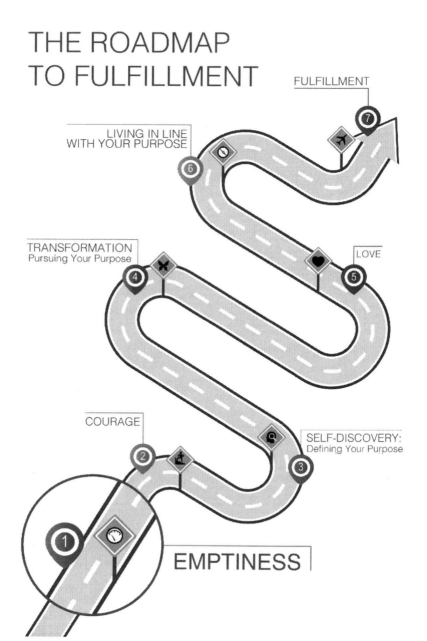

THE ROADMAP TO FULFILLMENT

FULFILLMENT

7

LIVING IN LINE
WITH YOUR PURPOSE

6

TRANSFORMATION
Pursuing Your Purpose

4

LOVE

5

COURAGE

2

SELF-DISCOVERY:
Defining Your Purpose

3

1

EMPTINESS

CHAPTER ONE
EMPTINESS

> If you deliberately plan on being less than you are capable of being, then I warn you that you'll be unhappy for the rest of your life.
>
> *– Abraham Maslow*

He was stuck in the same job for several years. It wasn't a job he felt suited him, but it was a steady paycheck and it had become easy for him. He was in his comfort zone and he had no reason to change. He would find justifications for staying in his job and maintaining his way of life. He did not realize that he was subconsciously making these excuses. A part of him did not want to change, although he knew eventually, he had to.

He went through life not really knowing what was wrong, but invariably feeling that he wanted something more. He would fill up his free time browsing social media, watching television shows, reading, and going out with friends, but it was not enough. He would distract himself, even create problems, because he wanted to focus on something other than the emptiness that he felt. Everything he was doing was keeping him in the emptiness, but he would avoid facing it at all costs.

She was immensely successful. She graduated at the top of her class, got a well-paid job, and quickly rose through the ranks to a top executive position. She was, by many people's definitions, successful, and yet she never felt as though her life was meaningful. She wasn't contributing to the world in a way which made her feel her uniqueness and worth, because she had aimed for prestige and stability, instead of focusing on the things which meant something to her. In the end, she was left trying to chase away the emptiness unsuccessfully.

Emptiness does not always shape itself as someone who is depressed or angry, or a person who is stuck in life, unable to achieve their potential because they are afraid. It can also look like the high achiever who is trying to find some answer to the emptiness.

All the money and fame in the world will not fill up your emptiness if you don't fulfill the calling of your soul. Without fulfilling your calling, you will always feel agonizing emptiness, even if you are living in a palace.

Emptiness needs to be recognized, no matter what "face" it chooses. It is responsible when you feel sad for no specific reason, especially when you are alone with your thoughts. It is responsible when you feel that something is missing, and it will continue despite your attempts to escape it and keep yourself distracted.

It is a feeling that we have all suffered from occasionally, which catches you by surprise, although deep down, you know why it is there. It is often an internal "wake-up" call to the fact that you have veered off your true path dramatically, and you're starting to become someone that does not reflect who you truly are. Do not ignore it, especially when you want to.

According to Viktor Frankl, a psychiatrist and the author of *Man's Search for Meaning*, individuals need to feel that they have meaning in their lives[1]. This can happen through four possible sources: purposeful work, love, suffering, and courage. He goes on to explain this by saying,

"A man who becomes conscious of the responsibility he bears toward a human being who affectionately waits for him, or to an unfinished work, will never be able to throw away his life. He knows the 'why' for his existence, and will be able to bear almost any 'how.'"

It might be that you have a family whose survival and growth you contribute to, or that you head a business, or that you focus on a charitable cause. You might be caring for a chronically ill family member. You may spend your time working on a great novel, or building a new machine. These are all ways in which individuals find the meaning they seek.

The Signs That Emptiness Is Looming

> Man finds nothing so intolerable as to be in a state of complete rest, without passions, without occupation, without diversion, without effort. Then he feels his nullity, loneliness, inadequacy, dependence, helplessness, emptiness.

– Blaise Pascal

The Pain Of Emptiness

Emptiness arises when you feel that something is missing; it brings on a sense of pain. According to Jim Warner from the book *Facing Pain Embracing Love*, pain can stem from any part of reality that we do not want to face or acknowledge[2].

You know that the emptiness is present when you look around and things that you thought had meaning no longer seem to matter. You feel that the actions you take are futile, and so are the outcomes. This can become more extreme as an increasing number of actions seem pointless. It's also referred to as *Anhedonia*[3]. You reach a point where your regular routine becomes banal. You pass the time without feeling alive.

This emptiness can lead to one of two things: it can

either bring you down further, or it can be a stepping stone to moving forward. You will know the emptiness is there; whether or not you push it aside is another issue.

The Allure Of The Outside World

How do we find comfort? One of the reasons that emptiness occurs is because we often look for comfort outside of ourselves. Although seeking outside comforts can be reassuring, no external force can provide us with fulfillment. You can only be fulfilled if you focus inward and try to be your authentic self, rather than spending your time keeping up the facade of your artificial self – one dependent on external pleasures.

In the hierarchy of needs created by Abraham Maslow, the term for seeking your authentic self and realizing your true potential is "self-actualization." It is something that we all strive toward and is one of the top needs of any human being[4]. It can only be achieved if it starts from within and is not dependent on outside forces.

The outside world can be perplexing and distracting. There are so many interpretations of what we think will bring us happiness – if we are successful, if we have a family, if we have nice things, and so on and so forth – that the list seems endless. Sometimes we think the emptiness will be filled by a fancy car, a new relationship, or a fat pay check. The truth is, these are just bandages covering the bigger issue. They are only momentary solutions that lose their value as time passes.

Most people spend their lives satiating their physical, emotional, and social desires. In turn, they neglect the needs of their psyches (their souls), and the voices of their callings, condemning themselves to a life of emptiness and unnecessary pain.

When I started my job as a CEO, the perks that came with the job were amazing. I was delighted by the luxury it offered, including a fancy car, first class flights, and seven-star hotel suites. After a while, however, those things brought me less joy and excitement than they used to. I no longer wanted to sit in a fancy hotel suite. I wanted to read my 6-year-old a story and see his eyes light up, even if it meant I had to stay in a shabby room or take a bus.

Even as they increased, the luxuries stopped pleasing me. What once made me feel important and gave me comfort felt more like a prison of my own making. I did enjoy the job, but it did not give me as much meaning as what I am currently doing, living my purpose of writing books about leadership and strategy and helping people and organizations create purpose-driven growth. As actor Jim Carey puts it,

"I think everybody should get rich and famous and do everything they ever dreamed of so they can see that it's not the answer."

I am not saying that materialistic gains cannot be helpful and enjoyable. Of course, they are! However, if they are all you are chasing, emptiness will inevitably loom, and it will trigger a deeper feeling of dissatisfaction.

That Is What I Am Supposed To Do...

> It isn't normal to know what we want. It is a rare and difficult psychological achievement.

– Abraham Maslow

When we are young children, it seems that our lives are already planned for us in many ways (name, parents, race, religion, education, nationality, living standards, lifestyle, etc.). Most of us go through school and at the age of 18, we are generally considered adults who are expected to make important decisions about the way we want to live our lives. Suddenly, we have to think about what we want to do with the rest of our lives – this is when the first adult "crisis" often occurs.

For many, it can be a daunting task. I have seen teenagers panicking, thinking that if they do not have it all figured out by then, they will live their lives lost in the abyss. The truth is, most people do not know what they want to do at 18, 25, 35, 45, perhaps even at 60.

It is not an easy decision, but at the same time, it is not something that should be scary or daunting. In fact, it should be an exciting moment. Ideally, when you reach the age of 18, you are suddenly free to step out of your zone of dependence and make decisions on your own.

Some people are forced onto paths they don't want to tread (by their parents, trends, circumstances, society, financial obligations, survival, insecurities, etc.). Emptiness looms when you aren't making your own decisions, and you do things merely because you feel obligated to. When you are forced or persuaded to follow a specific path, you begin to forget or lose parts of your true self.

Emptiness looms when you make decisions and choices that are not in line with your true self; you become a stranger to yourself.

A person I know, Dina, was pressured into a major that she didn't particularly like: engineering. Dina actually had a passion for acting and the theater, but according to other people, a career in theater arts would not pay the bills. Although Dina was an extremely bright individual, she hated mathematics and physics. She failed her first year of engineering, gained 30 kilos, and lost a lot of her self-confidence.

She ended up switching to interior design. Although this was not what she truly wanted to do, it was more acceptable than theater to her family. Dina's whole life had been planned for her. She later went on to do a Master's in Business Administration (MBA) and joined the family business.

She never got the chance to do what she wanted to do. Her life was hijacked, and she had to use her work and friends to keep herself distracted.

Try to imagine for a moment what would happen if one day she stopped and took a hard look at her life.

- What do you think she would say to herself?

- Is she living her life? Or someone else's?

- What would you do if you were in her shoes?

- How would you feel?

- Do you know someone like Dina?

This does not mean that she would always be happy if she had chosen her own path, but by following the calling of her soul and picking something that she felt brought out the best in her, she would be aiding and contributing far more. Being true to what she loved and playing to her strengths would have brought her motivation, positive feedback, and meaning.

You are both a physical and psychological being. If you ignore either element, you will suffer. It is your responsibility to care for your needs, because if you don't, no one will.

More Time, More Opportunities, Yet Less Satisfaction

Why are people feeling empty these days? For millions of years, fulfillment was about survival. The good life was quite simple: it just meant that you and your group had enough food for the day. Individuals were so preoccupied with hunting, gathering, and staying alive that they didn't even contemplate notions such as happiness.

As time passed and humans evolved to the point where

their basic survival needs could more easily be met, they began to have enough free time to contemplate and reflect on issues such as the meaning of life and the purpose of existence.

Humans strive to grow. We need to advance, and we need to find meaning. With all this extra time, if we do not bother to look inwards, the emptiness will begin to lurk and we will turn to distractions.

When a person can't find a deep sense of meaning, they distract themselves with pleasure.

– Viktor E. Frankl

Distractions, Distractions... A Blessing Or A Curse?

We have so many distractions these days. Many of us feel we need them after a long day at work, when all we want to do is shut our brains off and unwind – but what happens when the distractions take over and addictions begin to cement?

We have drug and alcohol addictions and, nowadays, social media addictions. We have become glued to television screens, computer screens, phone screens, and other types of screens, trying to pass the time. People joke that our phones have become part of our bodies, and if we lose or temporarily misplace them, anxiety begins to set in.

From Facebook to Instagram to Twitter to Snapchat, we have embraced social media as part of our cultures. This isn't inherently good or bad, but how we utilize it and how it affects our face-to-face relationships is crucial to explore.

For some, it has reached the point where they take a picture of and document every little thing that happens to them – to get attention and reassurance from others. For these people, it seems that nothing is enjoyable unless the whole world knows about it.

We live in a fast-paced society, where individuals are constantly seeking instant gratification. If we are on Facebook, we count how many likes our pictures have. If we are on WhatsApp, someone sending us a message means we are important.

The worst part is that although we live in a world where we are so highly connected – people are just one click away – it feels like we are further apart than ever before, and loneliness is on the rise. In general, smartphones are increasingly undermining social interactions. A report created at Virginia Tech University confirms this notion.[5]

Although distractions can be a refuge for brief moments in time, they are just Band-Aids; they cannot fill the emptiness. We need human connections, so we need to invest the time and effort to establish them, or else we will feel more and more disconnected and empty.

You can sedate yourself with alcohol, entertainment, social media, superficial socializing, and other distractions just to avoid the pain of emptiness, but your life will vanish into a blur of sedation.

Instant Gratification/Vitamin "No"

In today's world, many of us have access to things that we take entirely for granted, and we forget to appreciate these things. Some of us have, to some degree, become entitled, and this prevents us from enjoying the little aspects of the everyday that make life rich.

People who get everything they want as children without being given "vitamin NO," as family psychologist John Rosemond puts it, will grow up thinking that things come easy, and that whatever they request will be given to them without any effort on their part[6]. Soon enough, however, reality will "slap them in the face," because in the real world, things (especially things of value) do not come easily. Hard work is a necessity for success.

It seems to me that in the past, people were more easily satisfied. They took joy in family days out and simple gifts and gestures, while now, we are so over-stimulated that we can hardly process things. We are constantly trying to outdo each other in terms of gifts and experiences, and in the chaos of everyday life, we can barely appreciate these things before we have to rush on to the next thing; we expect constant stimulation.

A study on internet users conducted by Professor Ramesh Sitaraman, from the University of Massachusetts, found that users were not willing to be patient with the internet for longer than two seconds[7]. It has been shown time and again in the media and the news, and you may have even noticed it in your own behavior or the behavior of those around you, that humans are becoming less patient, and are unwilling to delay gratification.

Our relationships also mirror this. Partly as a result of social media causing shallow communication, and partly as a result of extremely busy lives, fewer people are able to really invest in building strong relationships anymore – and again, we seek easy, quick interactions to satisfy our social needs, because these are less work and give us an immediate hit of satisfaction, even if it isn't enough to fuel us for long.

Working hard for something – whether a relationship or a life goal – forces us to slow down, analyze what we want and how to get there, and then actually appreciate the thing once we have it. Delaying gratification makes the process more conscious, and magnifies the sense of gratification when it is finally achieved.

The most important factor which contributes to an overall sense of fulfillment is gratitude and learning to appreciate the things that you have. If you think things should be given to you, that it is your right to have certain things without doing anything, you will not truly appreciate or understand their value. It is essential for parents to teach their children that they will not always get the things they want in life, especially if they don't work for them. It is essential for each of us to identify things we are taking for granted, and to re-work our thinking to appreciate them more.

The Result

Both of these things – distractions and instant grati-fication – contribute to a general lack of satisfaction with everyday life. They prevent us from focusing on tasks and working toward goals, because we either waste time on ir-relevant things, or we expect our work to have an immedi-ately obvious impact, and give up when it doesn't. We jump to the next thing, hoping that will show instant results, and then to the next thing – and so prevent ourselves from ever committing to something meaningful and important. We also fail to sustain long-term, healthy relationships with support and time invested on both sides.

Our focus on instant gratification may also be why we seek happiness rather than fulfillment; it seems more achievable, and it is temporary, often stemming from short-term goals or random events, rather than the long-term efforts which will result in fulfillment. We need to be more willing to put aside distractions, focus ourselves, and work towards a defined, conscious goal which will make our lives feel meaningful and valuable.

For individuals today, seeking fulfillment is like look-ing for juice in the middle of the desert. Does this seem like a strange analogy? What I mean by this is that if you are in a desert and are unwilling to create a space where you can actually plant a tree, help it grow, and eventually pick and squeeze the fruits, you will not be able to savor the sweet-ness of its juices. In the same way, we want fulfillment, but we want it, like everything else, instantly –without actually putting in the effort needed to achieve it.

Fulfillment takes time and patience. The seeds need to be planted, watered, and cared for before they grow into a tree. You may need to work through turbulent times so that you can truly appreciate the calm that comes with fulfillment – the beauty and sturdiness of a well-nourished tree.

It will take a lot of strength to turn a life that is harsh into a life that is beautiful. It requires courage and resilience because just like the waves of the ocean, life will keep pounding you with reminders of its stormy nature.

What Triggers Emptiness?

It is common for most people to feel emptiness and confusion during the major changes in their lives, like the 18-year-old who has to make their first big decision about the path the rest of their life will take. We might also feel it while trying to re-adjust to life after a major break up, an academic failure, a financial or familial crisis, a job loss, a business failure, or a job transition. These are moments of great vulnerability, which can often leave us feeling confused and empty.

More severe instances can follow the death of a loved one, a traumatic event (war, sexual assault), or a betrayal by close friends or family members. These all remind us of how vulnerable humans are to aggressors and external forces. All of these events can shift the way you see the world. They can also highlight what is missing in your life and leave you exposed, with no distractions, and nothing to hide behind. These events are, no doubt, devastating, and can take a toll on anyone's life; it takes time to process them and move on.

Some people, after a traumatic event, forget what their hopes and dreams were before the event happened. They might even see those dreams as meaningless, because their whole perception will have shifted and become more negative. This is when emptiness can settle in. While this is normal, the key is not to let it move in.

Such events tend to push you away from your purpose because your actions will be driven by fear, disorientation, or anger. When emotions cloud your judgment, they may motivate you to do things that you would not normally do.

Life is like the weather – unpredictable. It is important to endure the storm and truly appreciate the sun when it comes out.

Feeling that we have no control over our lives can also trigger emptiness. **Humans always search for meaning; it is our way of making sense of the world around us.** This is how we function and protect ourselves. There is even proof that the brain will complete incomplete pictures because it does not like confusion. For example, if I write "eotinoms," as long as I put the first and last letters in the correct places, the brain will unscramble the word automatically – emotions.

Human nature attempts to manage the chaos; we seek meaning and order. Some people theorize that our entire existence has been an attempt to domesticate the environment around us, to be in control, and to feel more certain in an uncertain world. If everything around us was chaotic and meaningless, it would be difficult to feel any security. We do have one major advantage, which is that no matter how chaotic and meaningless the world may seem, we still often have control over one thing: ourselves – our attitudes, thoughts, and behaviors.

If you let emptiness overwhelm you, you will live your life with the blinds down all the time. Eventually, you will become numb to everything around you. Some people get to a point where nothing really matters, and this can end in suicide.

In *Man's Search for Meaning*, Viktor Frankl bases his insights on some of the most grueling times of his life, when he was forced to live in concentration camps. He talks about the importance of having some purpose to live for, and says *"Everything can be taken from a man but one thing; the last of the human freedoms – to choose one's attitude in any given set of circumstances, to choose one's own way."*[8] In difficult times, you have some semblance of control only over your own reactions.

In the end, we may not have real control over our environments, but one thing we will still have control over is how we perceive and react to the world. You can choose to look through the lens of meaning or the lens of emptiness. It is up to you.

Conformity May Be Empty

Emptiness can also arise from the feeling that we are not being true to ourselves. Many people fear repercussions if they rebel against society's expectations, even though the billions of us that share this planet cannot possibly all conform to the same cultural and societal norms.

On a biological level, we instinctively strive to be accepted by the group; it helps with physical survival, creates a sense of safety, and improves emotional stability. This means that many people compromise parts of themselves to fit in with the group.

In 1951, Solomon Asch conducted an experiment to test out the theory that individuals are susceptible to social pressure and, when it is strong enough, they will conform. In the experiment, an unsuspecting participant was placed in a group of confederates[9] (who he thought were regular participants like himself) and asked to state which lines matched (the answer was obvious, but the confederates all agreed upon a list of wrong answers).

At the start, the participant would usually go against the group and say the correct answer, but eventually, most gave in and just agreed with what the rest of the group was answering, although they knew it was blatantly wrong. At the end of the experiment, about 75% of participants conformed at least once, and only 25% never conformed[10].

This experiment shows parallels with real life. For example, consider how cultural norms are passed down from generation to generation. Many people, to this day, do not fully understand the reasoning behind many of the traditions they follow, but they follow them anyway. Approval of the group is a major human need, and individuals may go to extremes in order to satisfy it.

People will compromise their own unique capabilities and perspectives in order to be viewed favorably by others. This can trigger feelings of emptiness because, eventually, they will not recognize who they are anymore. Even the love and appreciation they receive will feel meaningless because it is directed at the image they are projecting, and not at who they truly are.

Every time you behave in a way which isn't true to yourself, you will experience emptiness. This stems from "you" not being fully you. Like Dina in the earlier example, you will be living someone else's life, which others have deemed necessary and proper for you. This doesn't mean that you must rebel against societal norms to find happiness; many individuals have lived authentic lives which perfectly fit these norms. The key is being true to yourself. Emptiness gets triggered when there is someone inside screaming to be seen and let out.

To be yourself in a world that is constantly trying to make you something else is the greatest accomplishment.

– *Ralph Waldo Emerson*

Connections Are At The Core

Another trigger for emptiness can be a lack of connections. Have you ever seen a couple who initially appear happy, but when you look deeper, you see loneliness and distance between them? They do not connect or talk to each other anymore. This can be one of the worst forms of loneliness because, although they are close to someone in proximity, on an emotional level, they are miles away. There is a lack of engagement.

This can also apply to relationships when the couple is continuously at odds with one another. Similarly, individuals who have no support system or familial attachments can feel empty, because they lack connections and a sense of belonging.

We have evolved as social beings, and depend on strong connections with those in our "group." When we find ourselves lacking connections with others, we will sense that something is missing. We may attempt to distract ourselves, or form shallow friendships, to mask the pain of emptiness.

That is why some people may feel lonely even when surrounded by a large group of friends: they do not have any deep, genuine connections within the group. Others may have just a couple of close friends and family members, but if the connection is strong, they will feel supported and loved.

How Do We React To Emptiness?

Do we bury the emptiness or face it? Imagine that your friend's mother passes away. You know that his mother meant the world to him; she was his rock and his support system. Instead of giving himself the proper time to grieve, he starts working overtime. He dives into his job and distracts himself from feeling anything. Is this healthy?

Most of us hate pain, and so we do whatever it takes to avoid it, suppress it, and hide from it. Emotions, such as sadness, cause us actual physical pain. Did you know taking a *Tylenol* after a heartbreak could actually make you feel better[11]? Our emotions are too strong to be confined to the mind. They are intimately connected to every part of our bodies. Almost no one wants to feel emotional pain, just as most people avoid physical pain wherever possible.

Run, Forrest, Run[12]

When we feel empty, some of us may react by running away from this emptiness – we distract ourselves. This is understandable, especially when you consider how much pressure we are facing day-to-day. However, the true problem occurs when we adopt momentary fixes as a lifestyle.

Some individuals will cover up the emptiness by diving into a relationship. They might feel that another person's love could heal their pain. Although relationships can be a powerful motivator, you are the only person responsible for your own fulfillment. Love can heal pain, but maintaining a relationship takes work, dedication, and sacrifice. It is not the easy solution many people mistake it for.

There are some cases where a married couple will have a baby to deal with the emptiness they feel. Many divorced couples with a child will tell you that they thought having a child would bring them closer together, but, in reality, a child will do the opposite if the bond between the parents is not strong enough. A child brings on extra stressors, and if there was a lack of communication before, it will become even more evident when the child enters their lives.

They Know Something Is Wrong, But Where To Start?

For some, the feeling of emptiness motivates them to try and take action. They go from venture to venture, looking for something that gives them a sense of meaning. They will be willing to try many things, but they will not master anything because they won't have taken the time to pinpoint the source of the emptiness.

The search for meaning is a long one, but if you look within, you will find the signs that will point you in the right direction.

For those who have the self-awareness to look inward, and who take the time to dissect their feelings, the sense of emptiness will trigger a cycle of self-discovery. They will start to wonder why they feel dissatisfied, and as soon as they decide that the feeling of emptiness is not what they want, they will begin their journey toward fulfillment.

Only by acknowledging the emptiness and finding the motivation to look for fulfillment can you begin your journey. The people who understand this have just made the first necessary realization. Next, they will have to find their courage.

This chapter was not meant to make you uncomfortable, but to open your eyes to all the potential that lies within you. If you related to any of the above, it is time to take the necessary steps and unlock your courage. Fulfillment is attainable; it is within your reach. Don't you think it is time to start browsing through your travel options?

Reflection

Indicators of emptiness can manifest in the following ways:

1. How do you feel when you wake up in the morning? Energized and excited, or lethargic and miserable?

2. Do you worry a lot? Do you have a high level of anxiety?

3. How much time do you spend watching TV, browsing social media, and distracting yourself? Do you believe this is healthy?

4. How would you describe your level of engagement and enthusiasm at work?

5. What hobbies do you have that you practice rigorously? How passionate are you about them?

6. What are you brilliant at and famous for?

7. How do you generally feel during the weekends?

8. How do you feel about spending time alone? Do you mind it? What kind of thoughts come to you when you are by yourself?

9. Do you feel lonely, even when you are surrounded by people?

10. How often do you get bored?

11. What beneficial causes are dear to you? How active are you in supporting these causes?

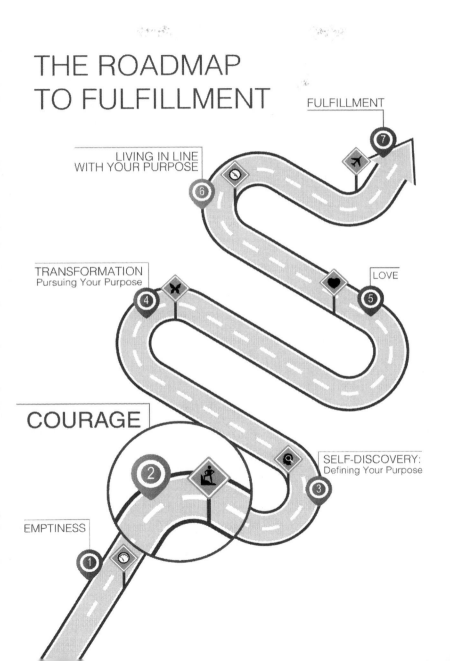

THE ROADMAP
TO FULFILLMENT

FULFILLMENT

LIVING IN LINE
WITH YOUR PURPOSE

TRANSFORMATION
Pursuing Your Purpose

LOVE

COURAGE

SELF-DISCOVERY:
Defining Your Purpose

EMPTINESS

CHAPTER TWO
COURAGE

All your need is the plan, the roadmap, and the
courage to press on to your destination.

– Earl Nightingale

Paulo Coelho's books have sold over a hundred million copies globally. Most people know him for *The Alchemist*. When we look at people like this, it's tempting to romanticize and envy their lives, but it's essential to remember that the journey which led them to fame was usually arduous and painful.

During his early years, Coelho knew he wanted to be a writer, but he grew up in a community where it was common to choose less risky professions, such as engineering. His persistence in writing and refusal to conform led his parents to institutionalize him in a mental asylum at the age of 17. Upon his release for the third and final time, he chose to satisfy his parents by abandoning his calling and enrolling in law school.[1]

He soon dropped out, and became a lyricist. After a stint in jail, where he was tortured by the military regime, he eventually turned to writing. It was not until 1982 that he released his first book, which didn't sell brilliantly, but wasn't a disaster either. He worked to stabilize his life, and was fairly successful, moving toward journalism as a steady career.

After walking a trail in Spain spanning over 750 kilometers, he had a "spiritual awakening." He realized that despite the success he had achieved as a lyricist, journalist, and theater director, he had given up on his dream.

"I was working, I had a person whom I loved, I had money, but I was not fulfilling my dream. My dream was, and still is, to be a writer"[2]

He decided to give up his career as a journalist and immerse himself fully in his writing. He wrote his first book *The Pilgrimage*, an autobiography, and a year later he released his most famous book, *The Alchemist*. Doing this meant putting aside a stable job, and going against the "safe" options his upbringing had pushed him toward, and he is now one of the best-known authors globally. He has changed the lives of some of his readers, impacted people he will never meet or directly communicate with, and made a difference to the world – a difference that he wanted to make. He did this because he was courageous.

When it comes to finding your purpose, there are two elements which nudge you in the right direction: the push that comes from not wanting to feel the emptiness and the pain behind it; and the pull of becoming your true self and wanting to make that beautiful and uplifting journey. The thing which pushes you in the wrong direction is fear, because the journey is daunting, and often contains many unknown elements.

Having courage will ensure you are brave enough to be guided by the push and pull, rather than being paralyzed by the fear. Courage will help you move forward despite the fears, insecurities, societal pressures, and other barriers.

If you look at the etymology of the word "courage," it comes from the root *cor* or "heart" in Latin. Courage relates to the heart, and becomes meaningless without emotion and passion. Courage is the virtue that feeds all other virtues, just like the heart pumps blood to all parts of the body. It is about speaking one's heart, because most of the time it takes courage to be the truest form of yourself. Many of us are not true to ourselves because we are not brave enough to be.

> **We all wear masks, and the time comes when we cannot remove them without removing some of our own skin.**
>
> *– André Berthiaume*

We place mask over mask, until we forget who we originally were. This is what happens during the emptiness phase; it takes courage to recognize that we are not living the life that we want to. It is scary to realize that you are unhappy, and it takes courage to know you deserve better and need to change. The fact that you are reading this book right now shows that you are choosing to embrace change, or at least become aware of your potential – which is a step in the right direction.

The journey will not come to you by itself. You must have the courage to decide, pack, and get on the road.

What Courage Looks Like

What is the first thing you think of when it comes to courage? Many people will picture a valiant warrior who is willing to sacrifice himself/herself for the good of others. Although this may be the prototypical example of courage, courage ranges from the smallest of acts to the largest.

Courage describes the baby who takes their first steps in an uncertain world. Courage is represented by the person who faces their stage fright to pull off a presentation they have worked tirelessly on. Courage involves any small step you take outside of your comfort zone.

Courage carries many faces. It is not about having no fears, doubts, or insecurities. It is about doing what is necessary to face your fears head on. Courage would not exist without the concept of fear, so courage, in its simplest form, is about mastering your deepest fears.

Nowadays, courage often requires patience. The journey to fulfillment has many setbacks in it, and we will need to have enough patience and self-belief to weather these, rather than give up. In today's fast-paced world, we have to be brave enough to wait for results, rather than expecting them immediately and doubting ourselves when it takes time: fulfillment doesn't happen overnight, so we need to harness our bravery and patience, and persevere.

You will go through periods of self-doubt and hesitation. You will be scared. You will face the demons of your scars, regrets, bad habits, and other negative thoughts. You need to unlock your courage to tame all of these demons and move on.

While you are moving toward a purposeful life, you will face many difficulties. There will be times when you want to quit and run back to the life you were comfortable with – not happy, but comfortable.

The lure of comfort is strong, which is why most people are unwilling to make this journey. They are aware that, as soon as they start, they will know that they deserve more and that they are capable of more, and they will have to step away from comfort and do something different. They will discover their potential to become far more than they are now and to create a much better reality than their current one: these are daunting realizations to make, because they demand action, and they cannot be ignored.

When you consciously say, "enough is enough, I do want to live in peace, joy, and fulfillment," you will be more willing to put yourself in the uncomfortable places you once thought you could not handle. Sometimes courage is just about the willingness to weather discomfort and wait for it to pass.

Emotions Can Be Hard To Face

One of the hardest things in life is facing your emotions. What does that mean? Every individual deals with situations in a different way. When something bothers us, some of us may get angry, some may cry, and others may just pretend that nothing is wrong.

When an angry person gets hurt, they start to yell, not because they want to, but because they are unable to deal with the pain. For them, yelling is a way to get rid of the pain or reduce it. Most people are unable to bear pain, so they expel it and transfer it however they can.

It takes courage to say, "I know this is going to hurt. I know that it will not be comfortable, but I need to face the emptiness because in the long run it will be worth it."

There may be moments in life where you feel like everything is out of your control. At these moments, being courageous and patient with yourself will remind you that no matter what happens around you, you still retain a certain amount of control over your own behaviors. Individuals who understand this fact, like Viktor Frankl and James Stockdale[3], who both endured horrific treatment as prisoners of war, have found the strength to keep moving forward despite the difficulties they faced.

Courage is understanding, even in the most uncontrollable of times, that you still have the wherewithal to control what you do and who you are.

Clear Indicators That Fear Is Talking

I want you to try an exercise. I want you to think about the past two years. Can you identify things which you really wanted to do, but which you made excuses to avoid doing? What were those excuses? Were they good enough?

Imagine if you hadn't given in to those excuses. What would have happened? How do you think you would have felt? Would you have been closer to who you want to become?

When an opportunity arises, it may be that you can find lots of reasons to ignore it, such as: "I will not be good enough," "I am not ready for this step," "I have too many things going on right now," "it's not right for me," "it's better suited for someone else," or "I don't deserve it." The main driving force behind these excuses is fear, and you need to have the courage to challenge them and examine the root of your hesitation.

> **99** Those who lack the courage will always find a philosophy to justify it.
>
> – *Albert Camus*

There are times when you don't pursue an opportunity because you genuinely feel that it is not the right step for you, which is a normal and wise decision. Remember that there is a difference between an excuse and a wise choice. Be ready to push past excuses and just try if there is no valid reason not to. Even if trying results in failure, at least you will have learned something from it. It requires self-awareness to differentiate between what is motivated by fear and what is motivated by reason, but it is worth the effort.

Before you reject an opportunity, you need to fully understand the reasons behind your decision. Is it because of fear? Will you require courage to pursue it?

Some of the most profound learning paths are the ones that follow on from overcoming a great fear. If you are faced with a situation that makes you afraid, try to challenge it and push on anyway. Once you start dealing with your new reality, your brain will work with you and not against you, and it will put all its resources into making sure that you tap into undiscovered potential. This won't always succeed, but this is where courage comes in; you must have enough courage to stand up and try again even if it does not work out the first time.

Use your fear... it can take you to the place where you store your courage.

– Amelia Earhart

Wired to Survive

Let us consider what stands in the way of fulfillment from a survival perspective. Our brains are not wired to make us feel happy or fulfilled; they are wired for survival. Anything that we believe may threaten us, emotionally or physically, will generate fear.

In other words, fear is the body's protective mechanism. Without it, we might be more inclined to place ourselves in unnecessary danger, so our brains will amplify certain risks to ensure that we stay safe. When our brains sense danger, they automatically shift to fight-or-flight mode, and release the same stress hormones as when we are facing a life-threatening situation.[4]

Your brain would not mind if you stayed in your comfort zone as long as that ensured your basic survival. Stepping outside of our comfort zones into uncertain futures may be perceived as risky, so we will experience fear even when there is no physical danger looming. In a way, this means that your brain is designed to work against your happiness, because true fulfillment only occurs when you step outside your comfort zone and challenge yourself to go beyond survival and head toward growth.

Courage can be as simple as asking the question, "What is the worst that could happen?" There are two possibilities: you take the risk and fail, or you take the risk and succeed.

Creating a better, elevated reality for yourself is tough, and the journey will be rife with fear, insecurity, and hesitation. Shedding your old skin, facing the pain of emptiness, and striving to live a fulfilling life is not going to be easy. It will take courage to accept that mistakes are by-products of the journey to fulfillment, and more courage to push on despite the setbacks, to learn from the failures, to get up when you fall, and to be creative when you get stuck.

It's going to be a rough ride. You will need to make big decisions and take calculated risks. This will require all the courage that you can muster, but doing nothing – living in emptiness – is much harder.

Motivation is often key to finding our courage. For example, if there was a pharmacy located in a dangerous part of town, the likelihood that you would visit this place is low. Why? Because you would be unwilling to risk your survival when you could get the same services and medication from a pharmacy that is in a safer neighborhood. However, if the reason for going to the pharmacy changes (let's say your child is ill and this is the only pharmacy with the medication your child needs), although it is still risky, the reason for going there takes priority over your fear.

It is in such moments that courage works best. The odds may still be against you – you are still facing the same dangers – but you have a reason to take the risk. You will not face your fears until you are motivated. Courage is about weighing your options and deciding that something is worth more to you than the risks associated with it.

What could be more worthy of courage than being yourself and living an authentic and fulfilling life?

Courage Takes Work

Whatever you do, you need courage. Whatever course you decide upon, there is always someone to tell you that you are wrong. There are always difficulties arising that tempt you to believe your critics are right. To map out a course of action and follow it to an end requires some of the same courage that a soldier needs. Peace has its victories, but it takes brave men and women to win them.

– Ralph Waldo Emerson

Courage does not happen overnight. In fact, sometimes it requires training, because your brain can be sneaky. At times it will convince you, wholeheartedly, that the reason you choose to avoid something is not because you're scared, but because you're smart. It can give you tunnel vision, so that all you see is fear, and it becomes paralyzing.

You need to be one step ahead and prepare a counter argument. Focus on the positives, the advantages of making this decision. Focus on the reasons you wanted to do this thing in the first place – care, responsibility, and self-appreciation. Try to argue rationally with yourself so you can make a decision that is not based on fear. Make sure you argue thoroughly and let your passion speak. Weigh your options and visualize the outcome; ask yourself: what is the worst that could happen? Is it as bad as I think?

Imagine the worst-case scenario: you fail. Consider what you can do to carry on. If it helps, you can remember a past failure and how you overcame it. In hindsight, was it as bad as it seemed?

Visualize the benefits of the outcome. What would your life be like if you were courageous enough to take a new opportunity? How would you feel if you altered your path, and chose to follow something that gave you meaning and lifted your spirit?

Sometimes your brain creates negative scenarios just to scare you (in an effort to keep you safe), and reality will often be far more positive than your imagination leads you to believe. Fight back and create your counter argument. It will help alleviate the fear.

I once had the pleasure of listening to Nelson Mandela's life story, straight from the man himself. He was describing the time when he was in prison. The warden of the prison usually tried to intimidate new inmates to keep them in line. He would yell in their faces, issue threats, and bring out the dogs – anything to "break" the individuals. It was overwhelming to hear about some of this warden's actions, and to imagine what Mandela went through.

One day, the warden came up to Mandela and stuck his nose so close to Mandela's face that he could see his own reflection in the warden's eyes. The warden started a ferocious emotional attack on him, which Mandela listened to impassively. Once the warden had finished, Mandela said (to the best of my recollection): "Are you done?"

The warden was taken aback by the question, shocked by his composure. Mandela continued, "Please remember that I am a lawyer, and if you cross any legal boundaries, I will make it my life's mission to make you pay for what you have done."

This made the warden flustered and angry, but instead of reacting, he left. Mandela then commented that he was relieved that the warden had looked at his face and did not notice his knees shaking uncontrollably throughout the encounter.[5]

Courage is not something you are born with. Most of the people that display courage are just as afraid as Mandela was, but they work to become stronger than their fear, so it does not grow and paralyze their actions. The key is focusing on the reward, the reason that you summoned up your courage in the first place.

99

> Nothing in life is to be feared, it is only to be understood. Now is the time to understand more, so that we may fear less.

– Marie Curie

Taking control of your fears is not just about being aware of them, but also about recognizing the specific situations that trigger them. Try to visualize ways in which you can maneuver around a fear, or look for better ways of handling it. When you are pinned against the wall and you feel that you are in danger of being overwhelmed, ask this one question: "What can I do in this particular situation that is within my control?" More often than not, you will have an answer.

As James Stockdale discusses this in his book, *Courage Under Fire*, it is not about being optimistic, because sometimes when you distort the truth and reality veers in the opposite direction, the disappointment can break your heart. It is about recognizing your current reality, and then taking the steps necessary to change it[6].

Life is not about making plans that you never fulfill. Plans must be followed up with actions. Dreamers sometimes dream so big that they set impossible standards for themselves and become overwhelmed by their fantasies. It's important to take small steps every day, to consider what you can do presently, and what steps you can take to keep working toward your goals. Don't forget to recognize and celebrate those steps along the way, and reiterate to yourself that you have the power to rise above your challenges.

*Do not let your thoughts and emotions overwhelm you.
Instead, try to master them.*

Fear will always be there, and it is not something to be ashamed of. Courage just means that you step up to the plate in spite of it. For most people, fear becomes a necessary part of their success story, of making them who they are. The next time you are afraid, remember that you may be facing an opportunity for growth.

Courage was not the absence of fear, but the triumph over it. The brave man is not he who does not feel afraid, but he who conquers that fear.

– Nelson Mandela

The Unexpected Obstacles

Sometimes the biggest obstacles on your journey are the very people you expect to support you. Naturally, we assume that the people closest to us – those who claim to appreciate and care for us – will be sources of encouragement and motivation. This is often the case, and some of us could not have overcome some of our life challenges without the support and care of others.

Unfortunately, in certain situations, people who should

support your growth will hinder it. They might coax you to stay in your comfort zone, demotivating you and keeping you stuck in your current reality.

Why this happens depends on the situation, but sometimes people feel threatened by the courage of others. If your behavior reminds them of their shortcomings and fears, they will try to reroute you to alleviate themselves of feeling responsible. They will envy you and feel disappointed in themselves, and it's easier to discourage you from changing than it is to take responsibility for their actions. By discouraging you, they make sure that you are stuck in the same boat as them.

Sometimes they may fear that changes in your behavior will affect your relationship with them. It might signify that you are moving on, and they may fear losing you. They will try to encourage you to keep up old habits whether they are healthy or not, because these feel safe to them. Involving people in your decisions and proving the relationship is still strong can help mitigate this.

It will take courage to stand up to those closest to you and continue your journey. The unexpected lack of support from your loved ones might surprise and upset you. If possible, you might choose to physically distance yourself from them. If you cannot, because they are important parts of your reality, then manage your relationships in a way that allows you to mute their voices in your head, shield yourself from their negative influences, and continue your own path toward fulfillment.

This is immensely difficult, and many people find

themselves sacrificing their journey because they don't want to do anything that jeopardizes their relationships. In some instances, this may be necessary; it depends on the relationship.

These situations are difficult, and you will have to negotiate them with care, but find strategies that allow you to keep growing. As a very simple example, if a friend doesn't want you to take a job in another city because they fear you'll meet new friends and no longer have time for them, reassure them that this will not happen.

Never sacrifice your growth for the sake of keeping other people happy.

Our Perception Is Our Reality

Building up your courage means believing that you can do whatever you set your mind to. In Martin Seligman's book, *Learned Optimism*, he claims that it is the way we perceive something, whether it is permanent or not, that makes all the difference when we are tackling a problem. If we believe that the problem will pass eventually, it is easier to deal with and will not lead to feelings of helplessness[7].

A passage that resonates with me comes from the book *Courageous Dreaming*, by Alberto Villoldo[8]:

"Whether we realize it or not, we are all dreaming the world into being. What we're engaging in is not the sleeping act we're so familiar with, but rather a type of dreaming we do with our eyes open. When we're unaware that we share the power to co-create with the universe itself, that power slips away from us, causing our dream to become a nightmare. We begin to feel we're the victims of an unknown and frightening creation that we're unable to influence, and events seem to control and trap us. The only way to end this dreadful reality is to awaken to the fact that it too is a dream – and then recognize our ability to write a better story, one that the universe will work with us to manifest."

This quote refers to our perception of reality. We each see the world the way that we want to see it. If we choose to see it through the lens of fear then that is all we will see, and we will attract that kind of presence in our lives. If we view it with courage, remembering that although we live in an uncertain world, we still have control over ourselves, everything becomes less frightening. We sometimes underestimate our own capabilities. Courage comes from the realization that we are the potential that we seek so hard to find in other things.

According to Villoldo in *Courageous Dreaming*, neuroscientists have discovered that our brains cannot tell the difference between the present and the past (when told as a story)[9]. This means that if you visualize the path to success, or visualize facing your fears, it actually makes it easier for you to keep moving forward. We have to, in one way or another, trick our brains into believing that we have done this before, and that makes it easier in the future. Take advantage of this and you will be one step closer to forming the reality you seek.

An essential point, however, is not just to imagine the end result, but the specific steps. By doing this, you create the necessary neural pathways so that doing it in reality is almost like a repetition of a rehearsed action.

Letting Go

 Some of us think that holding on makes us strong; but sometimes it is letting go.

– Hermann Hesse

One of the most crucial aspects of courage is letting go of fears, doubts, and all the obstacles that stand in your way. There will be moments in your life where letting go is the hardest option, but you still need to muster up the courage to do so and move forward instead of holding on and continuing to fight.

Let go of certain individuals who are bringing you down, re-route your plans, give up old dreams, and so on. There has to be some flexibility in your life because nothing is certain, and holding onto the wrong things can hurt you, waste your energy, and distract you from your true path.

This is where awareness plays a crucial role. You must recognize when to let go, and when you should keep holding onto something.

If you don't burn the dead wood in your life, you will not elevate the nature of your being and become that which you can become.

In Summary

It takes courage and patience to face the emptiness, and to understand where your fears stem from and why they became so strong.

Remember to focus on the potential within yourself. Learn not to settle for a life that is less than you deserve, otherwise you will never summon up the courage to push beyond and reach your full potential.

Denying the reality of a mediocre life will make you waste the possibilities of a great one.

The next step in the journey is to embrace self-discovery, to look into the mirror with no make-up, no masks, and nothing between you and your reflection. It is then that you can see all the parts of yourself, and learn to accept each one.

Reflection

1. Are you really satisfied with your life? Are you afraid of admitting that you are not?

2. What are you afraid to let go of? Is it really that important?

3. What is stopping you from embarking on a new journey? Is it really that terrifying?

4. Isn't improving YOUR life worthy of some courage?

5. Think of moments when you exercised courage. How did it go? Was it as bad as you expected it to be?

6. What is really scaring you about listening to your soul?

7. How can you outsmart your fears?

8. If you settle for emptiness now and then the worst happens, where will you find yourself?

9. What would motivate you to take action, overcome fear, and move on?

10. If you won't do this for yourself, who would you do it for?

11. If you act courageously and things work out well, what will change in your life?

12. If you don't act and life becomes tougher, what negatives will you face?

13. If the people you love most were in your situation, what advice would you give them?

THE ROADMAP
TO FULFILLMENT

FULFILLMENT

LIVING IN LINE
WITH YOUR PURPOSE

7

6

TRANSFORMATION
Pursuing Your Purpose

LOVE

4

5

COURAGE

2

3

EMPTINESS

1

SELF-DISCOVERY:
Defining Your Purpose

CHAPTER THREE
SELF-DISCOVERY:
DEFINING YOUR PURPOSE

> As no one else can know how we perceive, we are the best experts on ourselves.

– *Carl Rogers*

For a while, he stayed at his job because it offered a nice package with benefits. He was in his comfort zone. His life had always been based on adhering to what he thought would be the safest option. He used to feel like he could handle every situation that came his way, but then disaster struck.

His colleague and close friend betrayed him, and he was forced to take the blame for something he was not responsible for. After this incident, he was fired from his job, his only means of income, and he was devastated.

It became difficult for him to trust anyone. He started to doubt the intentions of all the individuals around him, and this drove a wedge between him and the people he loved. He became isolated and stuck in a vicious cycle of self-hatred and doubt. How had he not seen it coming? Was he that blind? Or was it that he hadn't wanted to see it?

His reputation was ruined, so finding another job seemed improbable. With no other choice, he separated himself from the corporate world and tried to figure out what he truly loved doing, instead of focusing on the benefits that a job provided.

With time, he started to discover who he was. Although the pain of betrayal had torn him apart, in some ways it healed him, for he found himself again. Before the incident, he had had a stable routine, but it had always felt like he was incomplete, and he did not have the time to look within and find out what was wrong – he had deadlines, objectives, etc.

He had also never realized how toxic his organization's culture was until he stepped out of it. He no longer felt like he had to watch his back at every turn. For the first time, he got to question things and think about what he wanted to focus on – what his life's purpose might be.

Life can deal heavy blows that seem difficult to come back from. It is in these moments that you make decisions that will change you forever. They will either break you or make you stronger as an individual.

Your initial reaction might be to see the world as dark, grim, and gray, but some of your hardest moments might be blessings in disguise. They not only shake your notions of who you are as a person, but also allow you to discover parts of yourself that you never knew existed. You may uncover weaknesses and strengths, and you might begin to question things, including who you really are.

In our darkest moments, we can either lose ourselves completely, or discover who we truly are.

Remember, self-discovery is like trying to figure out where you want to travel to. You are planning on buying the ticket, but you need to map out the details of your flight. It is time to do this and stop hitting snooze on the alarm clock that tells you something is missing.

Summon the patience and courage from the earlier phase and tackle this process one step at a time. You are not going to get to know yourself overnight. It is a long and slow process, filled with trials and highlights but, in the end, the journey is worth it. Self-discovery is about waking up from the dream-like (or nightmarish) phase that is emptiness. Just like in the Matrix, you choose to take the red pill[1].

"Knowing yourself" includes understanding what internally motivates you in the absence of external rewards.

It is easier to be motivated when your motivation is not based on something outside of yourself, but how does self-discovery help you find that internal motivation? When you learn to look inward, you will begin to understand what makes you come alive. This will motivate you to reflect your true reality, not one that the world is convincing you to adopt.

When you change the way you look in the mirror, you will be motivated to start aligning the current you with the authentic you. As the psychologist Abraham Maslow puts it, *"What is necessary to change a person is to change his awareness of himself."*

You Are Unique

To start off with, you need to remember that we are all unique. Each one of us is a combination of different genes, experiences, cultures, etc. No two individuals are the same, not even identical twins. Consider that the person YOU are will never be repeated; there will never be another YOU. You are literally and scientifically ONE OF A KIND.

Self-discovery will help you gain awareness of your true self and your uniqueness. With this awareness, you can examine your strengths and weaknesses, and explore what you want to dedicate your life to – what your guiding force is.

You may start to make conscious decisions to accept the parts of you that reflect your unique self and to filter out the ones that don't. This will further help you pinpoint your life's meaning.

Looking within will help you discover what you are doing right and what is working well in your life, and therefore identify what needs to be preserved, protected, and cherished.

Are you ready to examine and uncover your authentic and unique self?

Who Are You?

At an innate and primal level, I like to believe that when given the choice, humans tend to favor good over bad. Our core selves will look toward survival, growth, and collaboration, which in turn means benefiting everyone.

Did you know that a research study indicates that babies (who have not had the chance to be molded by external influences) are aware of what is right and wrong?

A study conducted at Yale University involved babies observing a puppet show with cut-out shapes, where one shape was trying to go up a hill and another was pushing against it. Next, the shapes would either help the climber or hinder them. At the end of the show, babies were more inclined to reach for the helper than the hinderer[2].

In a second round, the experiment involved measuring how long the baby would look at two different scenarios for. If the climber went toward the hinderer instead of the helper, the babies would stare longer than in the reverse scenario. This indicated their surprise when the climber, in their opinion, chose the wrong person.

This experiment can give us a hint at human nature. We have an inclination to help or to be surrounded by those who will help us, even before we have learned particular behaviors. We can, to some degree, differentiate between what is right and what is wrong.

Furthermore, the fact that the babies were able to watch the puppet show and understand the meaning behind it (as far as the experimenters could tell) indicates that even as babies we search for meaning and are aware of other people's motivations.

There Are Many Layers In A Layer Cake

As a person, you consist of two layers:

The first is the outer layer, which is the constructed self, the one that we have created in order to survive in an uncertain world. It feels obligated to follow the rules of society, and is the self that tells you that becoming a mime may not be the most acceptable profession, that you must wear smart clothes to an interview, and that you should eat with a knife and fork. It is the self that makes you choose a partner based on society's notions of what an ideal couple should look like. The outer layer craves societal acceptance. It conforms to what you think is needed, not what you truly want.

Although this constructed self creates limitations, it is also necessary, to a certain degree, for survival. It allows us to maintain group status, whatever group we belong to (e.g. family, community, society), and we have evolved to depend on our groups for safety and comfort. That is why we may hesitate to do something that will be rejected by our group, and we cling on to this constructed self.

The second layer, the deeper one, is the unrestricted self that encourages you to explore, grow, and seek fulfillment. It is the part of you that focuses on what truly interests you, and the person you would be if there were no restrictions. This is the part of you that chooses to follow your calling, whatever the costs.

For instance, if you love to cook, you may risk instability, uncertainty, and the comfort of a well-paying job in order to go to the finest culinary school. Your true self gravitates to the calling of your heart – what you seek deep within yourself.

This does not solely refer to your profession. Your authentic self is true to who you are in every way. It is true to the values that you stand for, and directs your actions in everyday life. In short, your authentic self is fully you.

In the hall of mirrors, you are everywhere. Which is the real you? Find your original Self, the one who perceives all the reflections and is amused by them. Then you will recognize your path and walk it, no longer stumbling over your many false selves.

– *Alberto Villoldo*

At times, however, it is difficult to differentiate between the two sides of yourself, because you may have focused on the outside layer for so long. Most individuals will convince themselves that the normative or outside layer is what they truly want – after all, society paints such an idealistic picture of what the perfect individual looks like – but the world is changing, and more people are looking to embody something deeper than this shallow outer layer.

The true versus the constructed self can be compared to real versus plastic flowers. They may look the same from afar, but when you come closer and inspect the differences, you will realize that although one is more fragile than the other, it is also alive and real.

The constructed self was created to withstand the turbulence and torrents of life, and that is why it is more durable. The true self, although much more vulnerable, is purely you. When you are in this state, you are beautiful as can be, full of life and growth.

The plastic flowers will always remain static, frozen in time. The real flowers will, at times, bloom to their fullest potential and awe those around them. There will also be times when the flowers will die and new ones will need to grow in their place. That is part of the beauty of the process.

The key is to try and align these two parts of yourself as much as you can. The outside layer is necessary for survival purposes; if you stick out too much from society, you risk being ostracized and isolated. However, no action taken by the outside layer should be in conflict with your true self.

For example, wearing something formal to work is something that society may require, and it (usually) does not compromise who you are. However, if your boss asks you to cover up something illegal and immoral that happened at work, this may go against your core values and compromise parts of who you are, causing you great regret if you agree.

Keep the best parts of the outer, functional layer that do not compromise who you are, but try to rid yourself of all the extra activities that you do just to "fit in." Make sure that no elements of the outer layer directly contradict your core.

Looking within will help you discover what the pillars which make up your life are. It will also help you see to what extent your current way of life is a manifestation of your real priorities.

Uncovering The True You

"
Can you remember who you were, before the world told you who you should be?

– Charles Bukowski

The first step to knowing yourself is spending more time alone. Try and reflect on your experiences. Which ones brought out the best sides of you? Which ones brought out the worst? What can you do to have more of the first and less of the second?

Self-discovery usually involves understanding our pasts, and how we got to where we are in life. As babies, we each have different temperaments and genes, but who we are is radically influenced by what we experience in life. To understand who we are, we have to recognize the key moments which have shaped every aspect of our personalities.

Some people avoid getting to know themselves because they are afraid they will come face-to-face with someone they don't like. They lack the courage to look at themselves in the mirror, so to speak. They are afraid that if they do go down the road of self-discovery, they might come to know their reality, and have to significantly change the way they conduct themselves in life. If you feel afraid, you need to harness your courage and look for ways to ease yourself into the process of getting to know yourself.

The Voices Inside

Throughout your life, you will have been influenced by the external voices of your mother, your father, your friends, your colleagues, etc. We are social beings and depend on each other to survive, and as we grow, each person we encounter will influence us in one way or another, creating micro-fractures in our beings, which shape our future selves.

Each person becomes a voice in your head, directing your thoughts, sculpting your actions. Some voices will be more important to you than others, but every decision we make is influenced by these voices, which we unconsciously associate with survival. We turn to them when we make decisions, and we rely on them to guide us.

The next time you make a decision, try to unravel why you chose that particular option. You might be astonished when you identify who is influencing you.

Which people do you think have the loudest voices in your head? Who encourages you to take a leap of faith? Who draws you away from reckless behavior and ensconces you in safety? Who discourages you from taking necessary risks? How do you make decisions free from the influence of voices? The first step is to recognize that most of the decisions you have made have not been fully your own. Think about who influences you, how they influence you, and why they influence you. Consider their motives and how you feel about them/their voice.

Despite the importance of many of these voices, the first step to knowing yourself is trying to become aware of them in order to be able to disconnect from them. If you recognize how their influence affects you, you will be able to make an independent decision about whether to yield to it or not. The self-discovery phase is about distancing yourself from outdated perspectives so that you can understand the reasons behind your decisions in the current moment.

Explore, discover, really get to know what you love or hate. What makes you come alive, gives you vivacity and energy and enthusiasm? Getting to the heart of these things will give you a deep understanding of yourself. It is important to differentiate between the decisions you make because of outside pressures (voices), and the decisions which reflect what you truly want.

At times, you may struggle to decide on something because the voices in your head conflict with each other. Somewhere amid them lies your own unique voice, the one that hasn't been tampered with – the unrestricted you – which follows your natural inclination. You need to start allowing that voice to speak up more.

What a liberation to realize that the 'voice in my head' is not who I am. 'Who am I, then?' The one who sees that.

– Eckhart Tolle

Have you ever been unable to relax because too many thoughts were racing through your head? Imagine those thoughts as different voices, and try to discern whose voices you hear. It is difficult, isn't it? The next time you make a decision, pay attention to the voices that run through your head. Who is your main influencer and why?[3]

Where To Start?

For most people, the concept of knowing yourself is not new. Many books, movies, quotes, and religions focus on the idea of looking internally and understanding who you are. Though many of us are familiar with the concept, not many of us know where to start. It can be overwhelming to even think about the process, and the journey itself is harder still.

It is perfectly normal not to know where the starting point is. The journey would not be difficult if we did not falter, make mistakes, and stumble. The key is to anticipate setbacks so you can recognize them, address them, and overcome them as quickly as possible.

To get to the core of your being, you could start by examining your habits, values, worldviews, and the "stories" you tell yourself.

We will expand on each of these categories briefly to give you a better understanding of them.

Habits

Most of the choices we make each day may feel like the products of well-considered decision making, but they're not. They're habits.

– Charles Duhigg

What we do on a daily basis helps define who we become. One habit that I enjoy, for example, is writing my daily reflections and sharing on social media after I wake up. It makes me feel refreshed to have accomplished something early in the day, and the habit has helped boost my productivity and sets me in the right frame of mind to continue on the same line. In contrast to this, there are habits that create tension or have a negative impact on daily life.

For example, a person has a habit of drinking a glass of wine every day after work. However, the stress at work has grown and they have increased their daily dose of wine from one glass to two, and then to three. Gradually, their after-work drinking habit turns into an abusive one, and that takes its toll on their life. They wake up late for work and miss deadlines. Needless to say, they have to make life changes, but it is not before they identify the habit and accept that it needs to change that they can work on improving themselves.

Try to think about the habits in your daily life.

- What three habits do you feel are beneficial to your lifestyle? Why?

- What three habits are standing in your way or hindering your progress? Why?

How you regularly spend your time can also be a good indicator of your feelings. For example, if you believe that you care about an individual but you make no effort to see them or spend time with them, perhaps the connection is not as strong as you thought it was. When we value things, they tend to rise to the top of our priority list.

What things do you regularly spend time on? These indicate your priorities. Your actions and thoughts make up your being; if you spend all day thinking about or doing something, it is probably a priority and an important element of your life. As Will Durant put it, *"We are what we repeatedly do."*

Values

In the simplest definition, your values are the cornerstones of your morality, and they affect how you make decisions. Examples of positive values include: honesty, integrity, perseverance, and kindness. If your current lifestyle matches your values, that is usually a good sign, as there will be less dissonance between the person you are and the person you want to be.

To understand what your values are, think of your idol – someone you look up to. What qualities do they have that make you admire them? These will more or less reflect the values and the character traits which you aspire to have. Along the same lines, think of your favorite city. What aspects of this city do you truly love? Why? This can also be an indication of what you think is important in life.

If you feel that your values do not really match your day-to-day actions, what steps can you take to align your values with your habits? Remember, you are unique, so what you value might not be the same as what others in your life value.

Worldviews

Your worldviews are the beliefs that you hold, the lens through which you interpret everything around you. They have a broader scope than your values, and refer to how the world works, rather than to what behavior is acceptable.

Some common worldviews include the beliefs that "all humans are created equal," "family should always be there for one another," or "hard work breeds success." Our worldviews are sculpted by our experiences in life, and reflect the conclusions we draw from them. A religion might make up your belief system, or your beliefs might be more individual.

Try to look a little deeper now; look for your underlying worldviews. Choose the first word that comes to mind when reading each of the items on the list below:

Life is	....	Money is	....
Love is	....	Boss is	....
Family is	....	Colleagues are	....
Relatives are	....	Spouse is	....
Mother is	....	Children are	....
Father is	....	Problems are	....
Marriage is	....	Success is	....
Sex is	....	Failure is	....
Men are	....	Ambition is	....

Women are	....	Death is	....
Friends are	....	God is	....
People are	....	I am	....
Country is	....	Past is	....
Work is	....	Future is	....
Home is	....	Now is	....

This exercise should give you an indication of how you view certain elements of your world. Consider expanding on the list, adding your own words, concepts, and ideas. The more words you consider, the better you will understand your worldviews, bringing you one step closer to knowing who you truly are.

The Stories You Tell Yourself

Imagine you were eating your favorite food and then spilled it all over your clean clothes. How would you react? What would you tell yourself? Would you berate yourself?

Sometimes our reactions to the small mistakes we make can be good indicators of how we view ourselves. Constantly criticizing our own behavior can be an obstacle in itself. If we seek to reach our true selves too fervently, we sometimes put excessive pressure on ourselves. Changing the narrative can really change how we feel about ourselves and others.

Making mistakes is part of the journey, so when you do, it is important not to say: "That was a stupid move," or

"I am an idiot." Instead, be kind and encouraging: "Yes, I have made a mistake, but I will be more careful next time."

Mistakes are a natural part of life and it is important not to let them overwhelm you. Look at them as stepping stones, a chance to learn and improve, and an integral part of the path you're treading. Don't use them to push yourself down, but rather look to them as a way to push yourself forward to fulfillment.

 Experience is simply the name we give our mistakes.

– Oscar Wilde

Think of life like a boxing ring. If you want to succeed, you are going to have to weather a few blows, and how you view those blows is critical. When a boxer gets punched, if their first thought is, "Oh no, how could I have let them do that?" this will affect their fighting ability, not only mentally but physically. Instead, the thought should be something like, "I will get through this; I can handle it."

Think of one or two mistakes that you have made in the last week. What did you tell yourself about these mistakes? Were you forgiving or harsh? Why? Consider how you would have responded to someone you love making the same mistake.

It is also important that you update the narrative of who you are. If you find yourself repeating negative thoughts that are holding you back, you need to alter those narratives to fit who you truly are. Don't allow false stories to run your life; instead, seize control and correct the stories you tell yourself.

Observing Yourself From The Outside

Imagine that you have a camera on you. If you looked at the video recording of yourself, would you like what you saw? Would your actions reflect your intentions and feelings?

Sometimes people feel compelled to prioritize things that are not important to their growth. Some people will make an effort to please others, not because they truly care about them, but because they seek their approval. It is important to be honest with yourself about the motivation behind your actions; you will gain a better understanding of what your priorities are.

I knew someone who would devote her days to planning activities for her acquaintances. She showered them with gifts and attention because their approval meant a lot to her. Her family, however, she took for granted, because she felt she would always have their affection. When she stepped back to look at this, she could see the incongruity of her behavior, and realized that her family had taken a back seat in her life, while she prioritized those she didn't care about.

It's easy for this to happen. Your days may be so busy that by the end of them, what you have and have not done becomes something of a blur. Important things can get brushed aside and forgotten in the rush of the everyday. To get a clearer understanding of how you spend your time and whether your actions reflect your intentions, try writing down some prominent thoughts or repetitive activities. These may pinpoint your habits and priorities.

Knowing yourself is about observing yourself from an outside perspective. We cannot always be objective about the actions that we take, so it's important that when we feel we are overreacting, we take the time to step back and view the situation from the eyes of a stranger.

For example, imagine you have yelled at someone for dropping a mug of coffee. You don't usually react angrily to such situations, so you need to pause and try to understand your response. Was it because you disliked the individual? Was it due to your boss having reprimanded you? Was it down to a personal issue? Such questions are crucial to ask when you have an unusual reaction to things. Try to view the situation impartially, as though you were a casual observer, and examine your behavior carefully.

- How do you deal with your emotions?
- How do you react to conflict?
- How do you deal with failures? Disappointments?
- How open are you to criticism? How often do you avoid it?
- What is your attitude toward helping your family members? Friends? Colleagues? Strangers?
- What would you say your strongest attributes are?

- What attributes would you like to remove or replace?

- What parts of yourself do you believe can be improved?

Asking yourself these questions, although difficult at times, can help you to look deeper and gain a better understanding of your actions. You will learn patterns and find ways to address negative habits.

The process of self-discovery must be done by you and you alone (sometimes with the help of people you trust or people qualified in personal counseling). Nobody knows what truly lies within except you, so you might ask for guidance from others, but it is your responsibility to walk the path of self-discovery. If you don't put time, effort, and patience into discovering yourself, little will change in your life, and your journey of fulfillment will fail.

You Are Beyond Your Thoughts And Emotions

I have always believed, and I still believe, that whatever good or bad fortune may come our way we can always give it meaning and transform it into something of value.

– Hermann Hesse

Life changes; circumstances change. One day you might be devastated because you thought that the man or woman of your dreams had broken your heart, and the next thing you know, you've moved on. Individuals tend to get so caught up in their temporary feelings that it becomes hard for them to see the bigger picture. At times, it is important to detach yourself from day-to-day feelings.

In a single hour, you may experience a hundred different things, from receiving an email to doing a chore like the laundry. Your brain is constantly analyzing and processing these occurrences using filters based on your current mood and past experiences. These filters will affect how you look at the experience. This will trigger a myriad of specific thoughts, which will then determine the way you respond in any given situation.

For example, your colleague ignores you when you ask them for something. You try again, but they do not answer. You might either respond to this by being offended – "How dare they ignore me!" – or you might feel more compassionate, and consider the possibility that they have something else going on at that moment.

Your perception of each encounter affects the way you react to things. If you are too stuck in your own head or your own feelings, you may neglect crucial information about the situation. In this example, perhaps the person was having a hard day and they needed someone to ask them how they were doing.

The aggressive response would be a result of you being too caught up in your anger to assess the situation properly, while the compassionate side of you would be calmer and therefore more likely to pick up on hints about your colleague's emotional state.

Feelings can also be an indication of your thoughts. Negative thoughts will lead to negative feelings, and vice versa. Sometimes the trick to changing your attitude is simply to re-frame your internal dialogue with positivity.

The process of self-discovery helps you with this very issue. Once you become aware of your thoughts, if they start running a negative commentary, you will notice and be able to inject a more positive perspective. This can be enough to turn your whole day around, and can help your problem-solving skills by giving you new ways to address issues.

Imagine you are at work and start to feel overwhelmed. The image of working overtime or being unable to finish plagues your thoughts. This creates panic and you can no longer concentrate because you start to feel increasingly stressed.

You need to stop the panic-inducing train of thought before you start hyperventilating in the corner. Move away from thinking about the overwhelming goal, and focus on finishing one section at a time. You will be able to celebrate each small victory, and you will have concrete evidence that you are making progress.

When you are dealing with a problem, it is better to break it down into steps. Focus on doing the best you can with each individual step, and then move forward. Each completed step will give you motivation to carry on with the next one. In the end, you will have dealt with the problem, and you will feel proud of your overall achievement because you haven't been ruled by your emotions.

It is your responsibility to control your reactions as best you can. You should try to respond to situations in productive ways that you can be proud of. You need to stop yourself from reacting irrationally (though remember that we all make mistakes at times). When and if you do react impulsively, use this experience to learn how to respond better in the future.

Types of Automatic Thoughts

There are many forms of automatic thoughts and you need to be able to recognize each one.

One type is an inaccurate or distorted thought. For example, "why should I bother applying to the job? I know I won't get accepted." This thought will stand in the way of you even trying. It is an inaccurate assumption about your capabilities. When you allow this thought power, you rob yourself of opportunities, and turn the thought into a reflection of reality. You don't apply for the job, so you don't get accepted: a "self-fulfilling prophecy."[4]

A second type may be a valid thought, but the conclusion that follows it is exaggerated. For instance, "I made a mistake in my presentation" can be a true thought, but the conclusion "I am stupid" is not. Some people are used to berating themselves, but this is a habit which you need to identify and break, because it will demoralize you and prevent you from seeing yourself as you truly are."

A third type is an accurate but unhelpful thought. This is where your assessment is correct, but does not offer any solution to an issue. For example: "this project will take more time than I have allowed" may reflect a problem you have, but instead of helping, it will only induce panic. You need to focus on the things you can control.

Recognizing these thoughts is crucial, not only for self-awareness, but also for understanding your emotions. As soon as your automatic thoughts become harsh, your distress levels will heighten, and your ability to function will decrease.

Reflect on:

- What messages about yourself are you constantly dwelling on?

- Are they benefiting or harming you? Why?

Imagine that your boss is giving you an evaluation. He mentions many positive things about your work ethic, the quality of your work, etc. However, as is expected in an evaluation, there are also a few criticisms.

Although your boss may have mentioned a long list of the positive qualities you have, these criticisms could define your mood and you might obsess over them, rather than focusing on your skills. It's important to change your mindset here.

Don't dismiss the bad, but remember the good, and make realistic plans for improving yourself. Constructive criticism is a tool which allows you to strengthen your good qualities. It should be seen as a means of self-improvement, and not something to belittle yourself over.

 We either make ourselves miserable, or we make ourselves strong. The amount of work is the same.

– *Carlos Castaneda*

Remember that at any time, you can choose to either see the world as desolate or as flourishing. Your thoughts define your feelings, which then define your actions. When you examine your thoughts objectively, you can choose whether to feed your negative ideas and emotions, or focus on the positive ones which help to propel you forward.

Think about the last time you felt sad or angry. What thoughts crossed your mind? Remember to take the time to unpick and examine your thought process, and ask yourself what your thoughts indicate. When you feel upset, re-trace your thoughts and try to understand what has triggered the sensation. Try to think of ways to re-frame the thoughts so that you no longer feel upset.

Understanding Your Insecurities And Emotional Hungers

As humans, we all have basic needs, and if we cannot meet those needs in healthy and productive ways, we will do so in less productive and often self-destructive ones.

When our need for love, attention, or nurture is not met, an emotional hunger may begin to form, and we will start to act in ways that feed that hunger – which contributes to the feeling of emptiness.

One of the main human needs is connection. The need to feel loved and secure exists even when we are babies. This can be seen between an infant and a mother. If the mother is not sensitive to the needs of the child, the child may become insecure and react badly when the mother leaves, or seek attention from others instead. This behavior can progress into adulthood, especially if a need remains unmet.

For example, an adult may do whatever it takes to please their significant other because they are afraid of being abandoned. There will always be insecurity in their relationships unless they address and overcome it.

Our need for attention and care is apparent even on a biological level when we are children. When you hold or carry a child, it boosts the DNA synthesis and growth hormone. When the baby is separated from the caregiver, both processes cease[5]. Our need for love and physical contact is rooted in our biological growth. There is a famous saying by the family therapist Virginia Satir,

"We need four hugs a day for survival. We need eight hugs a day for maintenance. We need twelve hugs a day for growth."

This desire for love may, at times, overpower the true self. Imagine that you are desperately hungry. Your body begins to focus on this need, prioritizing it over others, and seeking ways to satisfy it. Your senses may sharpen, and you might become more aware of others eating, or feel drawn irresistibly to the smell of food. The same intensity can be seen on a psychological or emotional level: when we are missing love and affection, all of our actions and thoughts will be focused on sourcing them.

This is when you need to be able to discern whether your actions are motivated by your insecurities and emotional hungers, or by care and love. Healthy, functional love is the best motivator for your actions. It is not based on insecurity, but security, so the decisions you make will be in line with the most authentic parts of your being, not parts that are striving to satisfy emotional hungers.

It takes time to come to terms with emotional hungers, but being aware of them is the first step in understanding your behavior and overcoming them. This is crucial in the self-discovery process.

Discovering Your WHY

Getting to know who you are takes time, but you can find clues in what you feel drawn toward. What do you spend your free time doing? Sports? Traveling? Reading books? Why do you choose those specific activities? Do they reflect a genuine interest, or are they distractions to pass the time, to satisfy psychological needs, or simply to numb your emotions?

Some individuals are drawn to acting or singing, not

because they have a true passion for them, but because they are attracted to the potential glamour, fame, and money commonly associated with such activities.

The life pursuits which lure your true self are ones that you would do regardless of compensation because you love them so much. Money should not be what motivates you. It is crucial that you ask yourself, "Why do I like doing this?" If the answer is not, "Because it brings me to life," "I know it will benefit others," "I am passionate about it," or more importantly, "it gives me meaning," then you should re-think your path.

The process of self-discovery ends with you deciding what kind of person you want to be. After you have delved deeply into your thoughts, emotions, and tastes, it is time to decide what you will focus on. What makes you <u>truly unique</u>, and how can you use this uniqueness <u>in the service of others</u>?

Once you have formulated your purpose, you will have the motivation to grow, rather than just survive, and this will in turn help your group to grow, which will benefit each member, including yourself. Purpose involves offering the best parts of yourself to aid the survival and growth of those around you. Imagine a world where everyone contributed to society by doing something that they loved in their own unique way.

Life asks of every individual a contribution, and it is up to that individual to discover what it should be.

– Viktor E. Frankl

I know someone who was passionate about thrill-seeking and adrenaline. He would try every extreme sport and leap into any adventure that came his way. Risking his life made him feel alive. However, one day he took a dangerous stunt on his bike too far, and had a terrible accident. He broke many bones, and was hospitalized for months. The period following the accident was one of the most difficult experiences he ever suffered through, with agonizing pain and a loss of independence.

When he recovered, he started to see his pain in a new light. He wanted to find a way to ease the pain which others in similar situations might go through. He took up courses and became qualified as a pain management therapist. Now, his days are fully booked because he is dedicated to every one of his patients. His love for thrills, coupled with this life-changing experience, helped him derive meaning from the pain and understand what purpose would maintain that sense of meaning: he wanted to help relieve people of treatable physical pain.

This work gives him meaning and a sense of accomplishment; he is able to make a tangible difference to the lives of others, to offer them relief and comfort, to give them a chance to recover. He can work one-on-one with people who desperately need him, and the energy and passion he has for these people drives him through 12-hour shifts, through forgotten mealtimes, and leaves him feeling fulfilled when he finally finishes his day. He knows he has had a positive, unique impact on those around him.

Defining your purpose can be difficult. Three key questions to ask yourself when seeking your purpose are:

- Is there a problem I am good at solving?
- Is there an opportunity I am good at creating?
- What is my special way of adding beauty to other people's lives?

It is essential to understand that "identifying your uniqueness" and "defining your purpose" are interchangeable steps, so one may come before the other, but both are vital.

What does "identifying your uniqueness" mean? It's about creating an inventory of the strengths, interests, and talents (natural or acquired) that you have. You should also include a list of events that have changed your perspective on life – both the painful and the pleasant ones.

This inventory can be considered the buffet of strengths, interests, experiences, etc., that you have, and initially you may just make up a sample plate to taste the offerings. Once you have tasted everything, you can select the foods which you enjoy the most, and put those on your plate ready for the main meal.

Focus your purpose onto a certain path that allows you to derive meaning, hone your craft, and grow so that you can share it with the world. As Abraham Maslow says:

"A musician must make music, an artist must paint, a poet must write, if he is to be ultimately at peace with himself. What a man can be he must be. "

Different people take different amounts of time to find their niche. Some people have a knack for picking up many skills. They may have tried many things in their lives, but they are stuck at the first round at the buffet table – they have not filtered out what truly instills them with a sense of meaning.

Some people do not even need a taster session; they know what to dedicate their life to, how to make a difference in their lives and in others', and they just pack the plate with it. Others may need to take a second, third, or even fifth nibble before they decide.

What Purpose Is Not

Before we move on to the next step in the *Fulfillment Journey*, it is important to understand not only what purpose is, but what it is not.

Purpose is not about fulfilling your emotional hungers. You do not become a singer just to be recognized and adored. You become one because when you sing, all else is forgotten. The feeling brings you freedom, lightness, detachment from other troubles.

As a singer following your purpose, you share your gift to bring smiles to the faces of people listening. You share your voice to elevate the lives of others. You would continue to share it even if it resulted in no fame, no money, even if it didn't satisfy an insecurity or hunger. Purpose is not selfish; it is meant to elevate the lives of people around you.

Purpose is not about competition. It is not about who contributes more, or who does better. Purpose is merely about living the most authentic and beautiful you. Competition means that there are winners and losers. When you are living out your uniqueness, you cannot be compared with others. Each person finds their own niche and provides something different, something that brings meaning to their lives. Purpose is about everyone contributing and working together.

Purpose is not about visions or goals. Purpose is a way of life: you always follow it. Goals have an ending, whereas purpose is perpetual, continuous, enduring.

Purpose is not about blind passion and motivation. Sometimes blind passion can lead you down a dangerous road that makes you hurt people rather than help them. Throughout history, dictators, tyrants, and cult leaders (to name a few) have been motivated to commit horrific crimes because they had blind passion. Purpose is about aligning your entire lifestyle with a cause or meaning that elevates the lives of others. Purpose is about guided passion and is bound by universally accepted values, such as respect, equality, or assisting others. Purpose is not about doing harm.

Purpose is not short-lived. It takes effort, and it is a life-time commitment.

Purpose is meant to unite people under one banner of survival and growth. An African tribe uses a word that beautifully describes this need for unity: "Ubuntu," which means "I am because we are." It is derived from the belief that we cannot prosper and grow without the help of others, and that we are in this together. We each have our role to play to contribute to the progression and well-being of everyone involved, including ourselves.

Once you have looked internally and gained awareness about yourself, the next step is to try and cement your strengths and overcome your weaknesses, so you can pursue your purpose and live a life of meaning and fulfillment. The good news is that having a direction makes the transformation phase a little bit easier to undertake – you know where you want to go.

It is time to let the plane do what it was supposed to do – fly.

Reflection

Before going on to the next section, let's take a pause to look back on some of the questions already asked, and a few new ones as well.

Deriving Meaning:

1. What painful experiences in your life taught you valuable lessons?

2. What events in your life put you on a path you didn't expect, but let you offer the world something meaningful?

3. What gives your life meaning?

4. What makes your life justifiable?

5. Why is your life worth living?

6. What calls you from within?

7. What makes your soul ecstatic?

8. What are the foundations of your current life without which your life would collapse?

9. What brings stability, order, and strength to your life?

10. What calling have you been suppressing because you were too busy satisfying your physical and emotional needs?

11. What kind of life do you believe would fulfill you?

12. Imagine your life as a glass filled with a certain substance and consider:
    • What is in your glass now?
    • How satisfied are you with its contents?
    • What would you like to fill your glass with instead?

Reflection

Examining Your Experiences:

1. Which ones bring out the best sides of you?

2. Which ones bring out the worst?

3. What can you do to have more of the first and less of the second?

Examining Your Reactions To Mistakes:

1. What did you tell yourself about these mistakes?

2. Were you forgiving or harsh? Why?

3. How would you have responded if someone you loved made the same mistake?

Exploring Your Routine:

1. What are you naturally inclined to do in your free time? Why?

2. How can you build on that?

Considering Your Thoughts:

1. What stories about yourself are you dwelling on?

2. How are they benefiting you?

3. How are they harming you?

Understanding Your Habits:

1. What three habits do you feel are beneficial to your lifestyle? Why?

2. What three habits are standing in your way? Why?

Reflection

Define the Obstacles in Your Way:

1. What aspects of life do you need to get rid of (dysfunctional habits, bad relationships, irrational thoughts, misguided values, inaccurate beliefs, etc.)?
2. What is pointlessly draining your energy?
3. What is stopping you from living a fulfilling life?
   - Is it reality or the way you are interpreting it?
   - Is it a commitment to someone?
   - Is it your fears?
   - Is it a habit?
   - Is it an exaggerated obstacle you are using to excuse yourself of your responsibility to be the best that you can be?

Exploring the Voices in Your Head:

1. Which people do you think have the loudest voices in your head?
2. Who encourages you to take a leap of faith?
3. Who draws you away from reckless risks?
4. Who discourages you from taking necessary risks?
5. Which voice influences you most and why?

Reflection

Key Questions to Define Your Purpose:
1. Is there a problem you are good at solving?
2. Is there an opportunity you are good at creating?
3. What is your special way of adding beauty to other people's lives?

Figuring Out Your Default Settings:
1. How do you deal with your emotions?
2. How do you react to conflict?
3. How do you deal with failures? Disappointments?
4. How open are you to criticism? How often do you avoid it?
5. What is your attitude toward helping your family members? Friends? Colleagues? Strangers?
6. What would you say your strongest attributes are?
7. What attributes would you like to remove or replace?
8. What parts of yourself do you believe can be improved?
9. What should you acquire to make yourself more resilient (new habits, beliefs, ways of thinking, values, etc.)?

Reflection

Discovering Your Uniqueness:

1. As a child, what did you love doing more than anything else?
2. What are your strengths?
3. What are your weaknesses?
4. What are you genuinely interested in?

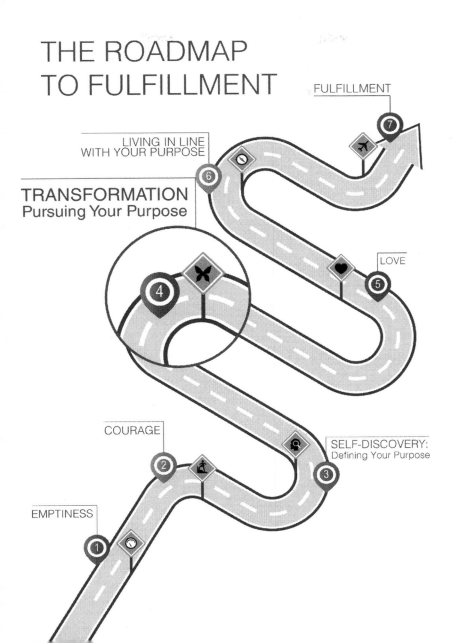

THE ROADMAP TO FULFILLMENT

FULFILLMENT

LIVING IN LINE
WITH YOUR PURPOSE

TRANSFORMATION
Pursuing Your Purpose

LOVE

COURAGE

SELF-DISCOVERY:
Defining Your Purpose

EMPTINESS

CHAPTER FOUR
TRANSFORMATION:
PURSUING YOUR PURPOSE

We must be willing to get rid of the life we've planned, so as to have the life that is waiting for us.

– Joseph Campbell

She quit her job at the bank and built a small workshop in a friend's garage. Everyone thought that she had gone mad. At the bank she had security and stability, a steady income, and good health insurance. Why was she risking all that?

She had actually put a great deal of time and planning into the move. She had saved up carefully – at times sacrificing things that made her happy – ensuring she had the funds and time to progress. She had tested the waters, selling bits of her handmade jewelry before she took the plunge. Everything had been done with care and forethought, and the change was not just on a professional level – it was on a personal one.

At the bank, she would see at least 100 clients a day. Interacting with others was not something which had come naturally to her, and she found it exhausting. In her own office, making jewelry, it was just her, her tools, and the limited interactions with the local jewelry shops who agreed to sell her items.

Owning her own business gave her freedom and self-expression, but the journey was arduous. She faced resistance on all fronts. She was afraid that her savings would not hold up, that she might be left homeless. She faced ridicule from her family and friends, who advised her to stick to the safer path. They said that she was too old, that the risks were too great, and that the reward would be minimal – yet despite the discouraging comments, she knew she had to make a change.

She stopped counting how many times she deliberated over quitting her job at the bank. The only way that she was able to find the courage to do it was by changing her perspective and believing in herself and her purpose. She understood that despite careful preparations, the road was going to be bumpy, but she was determined to hold her head up high every step of the way.

She tried to stay positive, despite the lack of support, and sometimes discouragement, from those around her, and the challenges she faced. The first year was the hardest; the business would not pick up and she was not selling as much as she needed to. All of the negative voices came back in the difficult moments, reiterating her fears. She had to work past them, past the calls of comfort and security. Despite all the uncertainty and hardship, she had gained a sense of peace because she was following a path that she had forged for herself.

 Don't ask yourself what the world needs. Ask yourself what makes you come alive, and go do that, because what the world needs is people who have come alive.

– Howard W. Thurman

The phase of transformation is probably the hardest in the entire process, the phase where individuals are most likely to experience setbacks and revert to their old ways. You are using the awareness which you gathered during the self-discovery phase to make concrete changes and move toward your purpose and the meaning it provides.

Getting through this phase requires making many choices that take you outside your comfort zone. It is about slowly, and sometimes maybe abruptly, changing your way of life so you can reach your truest self, and it begins with the willingness to embrace the journey.

Some people will not be able to deal with the resistance and discomfort, some people may change their minds halfway through the transformation, and some might not even start. You have to keep going and transform yourself, regardless of the turbulence you may experience.

 Life is an ongoing process of choosing between safety (out of fear and need for defense) and risk (for the sake of progress and growth). Make the growth choice a dozen times a day.

– Abraham Maslow

You will doubt yourself from time to time, even when you know exactly where you want to go. This is your brain trying to protect you from potential failure and restore you to safety, security, and routine. Remember that if you turn back, the same painful emptiness which sparked this journey in the first place will return. You must face the discomfort and the fear and continue on your path.

You must have the courage to say, "Yes, I am scared. Yes, there is uncertainty ahead. Yes, I could fail. But I am worth it. I am worth this journey, because at the end of the tunnel, I will be living a life that I alone have paved." You must have the courage to step past the boundaries of "normal" and do what you want to do.

To cross these boundaries can be challenging, because we are taught to handle situations by following certain protocols. When we do not follow them, there will be a clash between what we have learned (the constructed self) and our inner authentic self that is yearning to be heard.

We are all like Bonsai trees; our growth is limited by the boundaries that have been drawn around us – the rules and regulations we follow. We hide parts of ourselves, afraid of rejection. If we remove these boundaries and confinements, we become like the magnificent and giant Baobab trees, capable of breathtaking growth and extraordinary accomplishments – and able to derive meaning and find fulfillment outside of social constraints.

If you want a mental image of what this phase looks like, imagine a caterpillar's cocoon breaking open to reveal something much more beautiful on the inside – a vivid butterfly. At the end of it, people will ask you, "Has something changed? You seem... different."

You will be different. You will no longer be wearing your masks and you will have no boundaries suffocating your soul. You will not be trying to impress. You will just be you, and suddenly that will be enough.

Transformation is a time when you decide to create substantial, positive change. It is a time when you restructure and rearrange your life to create a new elevated reality.

Shifting Gears: Changing Our Perceptions

> **If you change the way you look at things, the things you look at change.**
>
> *– Wayne Dyer*

You create your own perspectives and experiences in life. You might be someone who relishes all the miracles of nature, from a spider spinning to a baby being born. You might marvel over the intricacies of a blade of grass, or wonder at the formation of clouds. You might brush past these things, and see only banality and emptiness. Which lens you look through will affect the choices you make in life.

Transformation, in its simplest form, is about changing your perspective in a way that supports your purpose – the one you define during your self-discovery. The question is: how can you change your perceptions?

How Changing Our Perspectives Affects Our Lives

Our perceptions can define who we are and how we live. It's important to understand where these perceptions stem from (self-discovery), and also to take the initiative to change them (transformation) when we feel they aren't benefiting us. We also need to make sure that the changes we make don't impinge on others' well-being.

Unless a person knows how to give order to her thoughts, attention will be attracted to whatever is most problematic at the moment.

– *Mihaly Csikszentmihalyi*

If you allow a harmful perspective to hijack your life, it will eventually reinforce itself into a pattern that is considerably harder and more disruptive to dissolve. Dysfunctional perceptions usually create bitterness and other negative emotions that would snowball and become oppressive and destructive. By changing your thoughts, your values, your worldviews, and your actions, and by becoming aware of your emotional hungers, you will affect your filters, and this will help you align your mind with positivity.

One way to start is to dissect the various categories (habits, worldviews, values, filters, and patterns) that you identified in the self-discovery phase. Gather information as to why some of these are ingrained on your character, and then address them. Find new perspectives that synchronize with your authentic self, and consciously prioritize these over the ones you feel are holding you back.

This step takes a level of mindfulness and self-discipline. You need to be fully aware of the present moment and your thoughts and emotions. You need to be able to identify when an old, default filter is negatively affecting your perspective so that you can challenge it and implement the new filters and, by extension, the new perspective.

Visualization is an immensely powerful tool. *The Self-Perception Theory*, developed by psychologist Daryl Bem, as reported in *The Guardian*, suggests that if you are feeling down and you push past the sensation, visualizing yourself as happy, your emotions start to align themselves with your imagined reality[1].

When you first wake up or before you go to sleep, take some time to calm your thoughts. Visualize the person that you want to become, your authentic self. Make them a reality that you can connect with, build their responses to situations, characterize them and embody them.

It is important that you meditate on this question of authentic self whenever you feel your constructed self taking charge. This may happen more than once a day, because we often run on autopilot, letting our habits direct us. Giving your authentic self space to breathe in the quiet moments of the day will make it stronger in the busy moments. You will become more aware of it, and that will help motivate and maintain the transformation phase.

Delving deeper into the idea of perception, based on Martin Seligman's book *Flourish*, there are significant differences between the optimist and the pessimist[2]. The optimist believes that, in general, the setbacks or problems they undergo are temporary and changeable. They believe that their bad situations are solvable and will pass. If they have marital issues, they do not take them into the workplace and vice versa – their workplace problems seldom enter the home.

Being optimistic prevents feelings of helplessness, because these individuals believe that there is a solution and that their current situation can change. Pessimists, on the other hand, view their situation as permanent, and their problems at work become problems at home. They constantly surrender to their negative thoughts.

To transform your life, you need to change how you see it. Altering your perspective will allow you to embrace transformation, especially through the ups and downs. As Mihaly Csikszentmihalyi says, *"We shape our life by deciding to pay attention to it. It is the direction of our attention and its intensity that will determine what we accomplish and how well."*

To support this point, let us consider a study by Richard Wiseman, published in the *Skeptical Inquirer* in May 2003. When testing the difference between those that considered themselves "lucky" individuals and those that considered themselves "unlucky," the experiment found that it was not environmental factors which mattered, but the perspectives of the individuals involved.

Those that were "lucky" tended to be more accepting of different outcomes, and were not decided upon one acceptable conclusion. When problem-solving, they could find multiple solutions. Individuals who considered themselves "unlucky" had a fixed and narrow focus; if they did not achieve the exact results they wanted, they would be upset and abandon the challenge.[3]

This section has summarized the power of perception, and it's vital that you carry this information into your own transformation. Challenge your thoughts, address your categories and filters, and synchronize your mindset with your authentic self so it can guide you in the changes which follow. Unlock your potential, no matter how hard it may seem, and transform your life.

Perfectionism Is Not A Way Of Life

Today's world can be uncomfortably competitive and stressful, and this is often down to the fact that we are striving for "competitive perfection." It is easy to get sucked into what the "ideal" life looks like, and to prioritize it over everything else. Based on the book *Being Happy*, by Tal Ben-Shahar, one of the core obstacles standing in the way of happiness (or in our case fulfillment) is our need for the illusion of perfection[4].

This desire for perfection may be partially responsible for the abandonment of many new projects. Our need for instant success limits our ability to accept the initial failures that are inevitable when starting something new. Many individuals will not venture far from their comfort zones because they are afraid of not meeting their own unrealistic expectations of what their lives should look like. We have to accept that things will take time, and that mistakes and "imperfections" are integral parts of any process.

Few people have the patience for failure anymore. When you tackle a project with the mentality that it must be perfect, you will be unable to complete it. You need to work with what you have and make the most of it, accepting that perfection rarely – if ever – exists in reality. If you set your standards too high, you will quickly become discouraged and revert back to your old habits.

As an example, let's consider a woman called Rachel. Her job was to ensure that the company she worked for was using its resources efficiently. She would analyze the books in painstaking detail, looking for anywhere they could save money. She was undoubtedly meticulous, but also highly inefficient. She was so focused on capturing every detail that a task which could have been completed in mere hours would take her days. Any savings she made weren't enough to cover the lost time.

Eventually, Rachel was demoted and put in charge of writing briefs and photocopying documents. However, this also took her too long, and she would sometimes rewrite briefs to ensure they were perfect. She was too focused on insignificant details to see the impact she was having on the bigger picture. Thankfully, she eventually got some perspective and realized that important things were getting neglected for the sake of immaterial adjustments.

Tal Ben-Shahar proposes another form of perfectionism – optimalism – where a person works within the constraints of their reality and adapts to the changing circumstances. While perfectionists have a particular vision – which is usually unrealistic – and the end result needs to match up to their plan, an *optimalist* does not limit their vision, and can easily adapt to the circumstances around them[5].

Let's now apply this to our goal of reaching fulfillment. Being fulfilled is not about creating a perfect life with every detail laid out. Fulfilled people have a framework for where they want to be, not a detailed plan. They adapt their framework to suit their reality.

Prioritize: Don't Lose Sight Of What Is Important

Transformation is hard and life is unpredictable. If you are committed to your journey of fulfillment, you need to step up; nothing will happen if you don't act. It's time you decide where to start and what to prioritize.

Have there been moments when you found yourself stuck because you were focused on too many things? I believe that one of the hardest things in life is to set your priorities and focus on what is important. Sometimes we try to take on more than we can handle, but the key is prioritizing. Our lives are made up of a series of decisions about where we will put our focus.

In this phase you must consider what is important – allowing your authentic and beautiful self to shine. When you focus on insignificant details, you lose sight of what you truly want to do.

Instead, you should build a framework around your aspirations and your purpose. Use this framework to shape your day-to-day activities. Be open to different paths and techniques which will help you achieve your purpose, and utilize your strengths to get through good and bad situations with the best possible outcome. Remember, there is more than one way of achieving a goal.

If you feel that you are immersing yourself in unimportant details, take a step back, revise your framework, and adjust your path. Do not get distracted by what you are missing, but focus on your strengths and what you can do with them.

Celebrate the successes, learn from the failures, and be satisfied with your achievements. Do not nitpick them until you are disappointed in everything. The sensation of fulfillment depends on feeling satisfied, and – as we have discussed – most of this is down to your perspective.

If it helps, you can write your framework down and review it regularly to make sure you maintain your focus. This will help you avoid perfectionism and allow you to adapt to any change in your reality without sacrificing your priorities.

You Are Your Habits

We discussed habits in the self-discovery section, but only in terms of identifying bad habits. Now we are going to look at how you can deal with them. Habits are essential and affect all aspects of your life. They are your usual way of behaving, what you normally do on a daily basis, and with time they become a part of who you are.

Your actions reflect your lifestyle, so you must choose your habits wisely. When a habit is repeated frequently enough, it becomes ingrained and can re-wire your brain so that you do it automatically, without rationalizing or questioning it. This is when harmful habits become dangerous.

The "Habit Loop"

A part of transformation is controlling or changing your harmful habits. To help you address harmful habits, let's look at the concept of a "habit loop," which Charles Duhigg explores in his book *The Power of Habit.*

The "habit loop" has three stages: cue, routine, and reward. The **cue** initiates the process, prompting action from the individual. You must identify cues if you want to understand what has formed the habit, and what the habit is a response to (e.g. stress might trigger the desire for a cigarette).

Next comes the **routine** – the habit itself, the action which you take in response to the cue.

The last stage is the **reward**. If the habit is worth repeating, it will continuously be reinforced, and that is how it becomes a regular part of your life. The key to changing your habits lies in understanding this loop and being able to either remove the reward or change the way you react to the cue or the reward[6].

In one way or another, your brain starts to rely on the reward that this habit produces. As Duhigg puts it, *"To change an old habit, you must address an old craving. You have to keep the same cues and rewards as before and feed the craving by inserting a new routine."*

Think about individuals who bite their nails. If their cue to bite their nails is a stressful situation and the reward is momentary relaxation, their reward system is powerful. There are many stressful situations in life, so if they connect the nail-biting with reduced stress then it will be continuously present. If, instead, they took up another habit in order to reap the same benefits, this could help challenge their nail-biting. For example, they might try deep breathing techniques as a response to stress, removing the need to bite their nails.

In most cases, focusing on why you have a specific habit and replicating the cue and reward in a different way can make it easier to change the habit.

Changing a habit takes self-control and self-belief. There are some habits that, when you start to change them, can dislodge others and create transformational changes.

For example, making an early bedtime one of your habits can change the way your entire day is structured. Imagine that you usually stay up late, wake up late, and barely make it to work on time. One day, you decide to rework your sleeping pattern, and the course of your entire day shifts accordingly. You will have more time for the activities that you would normally pass up in the rush to get to work. You might start to exercise in the mornings, which in turn could influence your eating habits. A simple change like going to bed earlier can shift many other habits and take you a step closer to becoming who you want to become.

In Nir Eyal's book *Hooked*, a fourth step was added to the "habit loop" – investment[7]. The more time and effort you put into something, the more likely you are to get hooked into it. For example, if someone has been practicing the piano every morning for five years, the chances of them dropping the habit are less than for someone who has only practiced for one year. The five-year investment of time and effort will reinforce the behavior and ensure they continue this habit.

When trying to establish new, healthier habits, such as waking up early, consider investing money in a morning activity that you enjoy. This may make you more motivated, because you have given yourself something new and exciting, and put something of value into pursuing the habit.

How do we avoid slipping back into bad habits? Awareness is key. If you know the triggers in your environment, you can try and avoid them. If they cannot be avoided, it is important to look for alternative habits that reap the same rewards, and invest in them so that they stick.

The only person you are destined to become is the person you decide to be.

– Ralph Waldo Emerson

143

Taking It One Step At A Time

When trying to implement changes, start small. If you take on too much, the likelihood of failure increases. Don't leap out of your comfort and safety zone, but step out. Change one habit, and once that has become part of your routine, change another. Celebrate your successes, and make sure the new rewards are at least as effective as the old ones.

Once you have decided which habit you want to change and come up with a strategy for changing it, you must commit and follow through. Many people know what they need to do and how to do it, but lack the initiative, courage, or motivation to start. That is why courage is one of the essential parts of the model; it pushes you through the difficult steps, making the whole endeavor less daunting.

Approach new habits sensibly to maximize your chances of success. If you want to learn Spanish, for example, choose a realistic amount of time to put into it. If you make it easy for yourself, you are more likely to do it, and you will reap the benefits of continual effort, rather than intense attempts which burn you out because they aren't compatible with your lifestyle.

Obstacles You May Come Across

I can't change the direction of the wind, but I can adjust my sails to always reach my destination.

– Jimmy Dean

Your environment will have an enormous impact on your habits and ability to change.

Imagine that you have an anger management issue, and you have made the active decision to try and tone down your temper. You opt for taking a deep breath before you respond to something so you can avoid snap reactions. Be prepared for your patience to be tested every step of the way, and incidents to "cue" your habitual angry response.

For instance, if you are driving your car and someone behind you starts to honk their horn, this may trigger frustration. Alternatively, if your boss is in a bad mood and takes it out on you, you might start to respond aggressively.

In one way or another, our environments are constantly presenting us with situations that can push us off our original course. In Joseph Campbell's book *Pathways to Bliss*, he explores how even small everyday tasks can pull you down if you let them[8]. Instead of seeing mundane tasks as a burden, try to find their value and importance, or turn them into something valuable to your daily routine. You might incorporate meditation into your dish-washing routine, or sing while you clean the windows. Giving tasks energy and enjoyment makes them easier.

Know Your Triggers

Marshall Goldsmith and Mark Reiter, authors of the book *Triggers*, focus on how specific triggers in certain environments may push an individual off track[9]. Ideally, you should try and avoid situations that you feel may trigger maladaptive behavior. If you cannot, brainstorm ways you can avoid having a negative response.

To do this, it is crucial to visualize yourself handling the situation well, and to try and deal with any resentment, anger, or sadness you may feel beforehand.

Imagine that you have a colleague who brings out the worst side of you. She pushes your buttons and whenever you are forced to be in the same room as her, there is an argument. If this individual cannot be avoided because they are in your workplace, it is important to identify the reasons you find her aggravating. Is there an unspoken rivalry between you? Does she seem proud or condescending?

Whatever the reason, understand it, and then try to separate it from yourself. If you feel that your colleague is simply an arrogant person, you can avoid getting flustered by this behavior by remembering that she is like that with everyone, and it says more about her character than yours. However, if she targets you specifically then you may need to have a discussion about the issues and boundaries in your relationship.

The aspects of your life that you want to change will vary in their difficulty and the amount of control you have over them. Some changes will be entirely down to you. If, for example, you want to lose weight, there are clear steps to follow and your success is dependent on your own actions. On the other hand, improving your relationship with your colleagues will be at least partially dependent on their actions as well as your own.

This is why, when you are dealing with different triggers, you need to remember that you cannot control every aspect of the situation. All you can control is how you react and whether or not you take things personally. When you find yourself facing a trigger-filled situation, think back to the question, "what would my idol do?" and act accordingly, or you will have taken a step away from fulfillment, and jeopardized your transformation.

Our environment makes our journeys much harder, throwing unexpected situations, setbacks, distractions, expectations, and obstacles in our way. Discipline is crucial at this stage. It is no longer just about knowing what you want and making a plan, but about sticking to that plan every step of the way.

Be Wary Of Your Thoughts

Your thoughts can be your greatest allies or your worst enemies. You need to control them as much as you can. When you are trying to focus on a task in front of you but find that your thoughts have spilled over into next week's schedule, you need to re-route and regain control. First, you need to be aware that you have lost control and, second, you must create a sense of urgency in order to shift your attention back to the task at hand.

In the book *The 15 Invaluable Laws of Growth*, John Maxwell suggests that each morning you repeat the following: "Do it now, do it now, do it now."[10] In Arabic, there is a saying that goes "do not delay what you can do today until tomorrow," because when that happens, we slip, and things that were supposed to happen weeks ago haven't even been started.

An excellent way to clear your mind and disconnect from unnecessary noise is meditation. It can help you focus on what is truly important, and brush aside some of the things which are sucking up your time without reciprocating with meaning.

Based on the book *The Power of Myth*, sometimes it helps to have your own special place to retreat to. You can spend a bit of time disconnecting, and focusing on your positive attributes, rather than the things you dislike. Detach from the noise of your environment and realign your thoughts with positivity if they have slipped[11]. As Hermann Hesse said, *"Within you there is a stillness and sanctuary to which you can retreat at any time and be yourself."*

Moving From Comfort to Discomfort

> *Life begins at the end of your Comfort Zone.* So if you're feeling uncomfortable right now, know that the change taking place in your life is a *beginning*, not an ending.

– Neale Donald Walsch

We know from the previous chapters that fear tends to keep us in our comfort and safety zones, even when we realize that we are not satisfied. To address this, we have to think about changes. If you are not happy with the current state of affairs in your life, what approach can you take? Why are you stagnating instead of growing? It is time to look deep within and understand the hidden payoffs that you are receiving.

When I discuss payoffs, I mean the rewards you get for staying in a job that bores you, or remaining with a partner who doesn't suit you. What benefit do you get when you compromise on fulfillment? Are you prioritizing money, security, flexibility, working hours? Is the reward companionship over potential loneliness?

Based on Jim Warner's *Facing Pain Embracing Love*, we are pulled between two competing urges: pain and love[12]. Many people will deny or resist them, and get stuck in a place that does not resemble their authentic self. The only way to reach authentic living is to experience the pain (undergo transformation) at the same time as embracing love. If we deny the pain and try to resist it, we close ourselves off to other vital emotions such as love.

Think of emotions as water coming from a tap. If you turn off the tap, nothing will flow. You won't feel pain, but you also won't feel love, joy, happiness, etc. Discomfort is natural and necessary. Being fulfilled is about accepting the negative as well as the positive.

It is crucial to understand that we need to experience pain as a part of life, although if we stay too long in the pain, resulting in suffering, it becomes dysfunctional and problems arise. We must learn to go through the pain, but to move past it before it overwhelms us.

Think of yourself as a seed. Although you can remain a seed forever, it's unlikely that you would choose this over the opportunity to sprout and grow. To become the plant, you must tear through your seed casing, or you will be living your life shielded and contained, losing your potential to sprout and flourish. As the humanist psychologist Rollo May put it, "One does not become fully human painlessly."

Transformation is a time where you will experience intense internal resistance (fear and pain), and probably external resistance (people who want you to stay as you are, and your environment which puts pressure on you). Remain steadfast, plan carefully, summon your courage and resolve, and push forward to fulfillment.

Moving From The Current To The Ideal

You are extraordinary within your limits, but your limits are extraordinary!

– Gertrude Stein

After discovering who you are and what path you want to follow, it is important not to get discouraged by the length of the journey. However, you must make sure that your ideal self is attainable and realistic; we cannot aspire (beyond the metaphorical) to grow wings and fly like a bird when we don't have the physical capacity to do so, and we must recognize this.

Thinking big is beautiful. However, it has a downside: when you expect too much of yourself, you will inevitably be disappointed, and may start to doubt your own capabilities.

We must recognize our limitations but utilize our ultimate weapon – creativity. We know that our bodies are not physically made to fly, so we create contraptions that can. On the journey, we have to be prepared to "fall" and sustain a few injuries, but as long as our goals are realistic, we will progress.

If you are aiming for something unrealistic, go back to the drawing board and find something you know you can achieve if you put your mind to it. Focus on your strengths, your resources, and your current capabilities; these can give you a good idea where to start.

Being Grateful

Sometimes we get so caught up in our own worlds that we forget to look around and appreciate what we have. There are moments when things seem dark – think of the times when people get fired and it jeopardizes their families, or when a person loses a loved one in a tragic accident.

We have to address and experience the anger or sadness caused by these moments in order to move on from them. When you have allowed the emotion some time, step back and be thankful for the things that you are still blessed with in life. If you can, try to think about what you can salvage and what you still have.

This is not easy, and in some extremely difficult situations, it might seem impossible. However, you have to try to the best of your ability to appreciate what you still have, and to see how you can make the best out of your situation.

Being grateful is one of the most essential steps on the path to fulfillment. How can you ever be satisfied if you do not appreciate what you currently have? One exercise that may prove beneficial is to spend a few minutes every day, especially when you wake up and before you go to sleep, thinking about the things you are grateful for. In times of uncertainty or difficulty, which may sometimes be a by-product of the transformation phase, feeling gratitude can give you the push that you need to keep moving forward.

There are so many small things in life that we tend to take for granted. Motivational speaker Nick Vujicic gives individuals a different perspective on what it means to be grateful. He was born with no legs or arms, and yet he is living life to the fullest and inspiring millions on his way[13].

Are you healthy? There are so many people out there fighting terrible, debilitating diseases.

Do you have a loving caregiver? There are many who are orphaned.

Do you have a job that pays the bills? Many others are struggling with unemployment.

The simple fact that you are able to read is something to be grateful for. When you are feeling down, it is important not to focus on the things that are missing from your life, or the things that are going wrong, but on the things you do have, and the things that are going your way. Be thankful for all the little things, like food, health, shelter, family, friends, etc., and remind yourself of them. Do not take them for granted.

Forgiving

Forgiveness is really a gift to yourself – have the compassion to forgive others, and the courage to forgive yourself.

– Mary Anne Radmacher

153

Your biggest enemy is often yourself. It can be hard to forgive someone who has hurt you, but it can take considerably more courage and strength to forgive yourself.

Guilt, shame, regret, anger, and other emotions may often require forgiveness for you to let them go. You need to confront the emotions, embrace them, and find ways to move past them.

Sometimes, when these emotions take hold of us, they pull us down and keep us stuck. If you want to transform yourself and your life, to move from your constructed self to your authentic and beautiful self, you must release yourself from the bondage of these emotions.

However, there are times when these emotions might be the spark that lights the fire of change during the transformation phase. When you mess up and hurt others (or yourself), these emotions are justified; they motivate you to set things right, and to redeem yourself and justify self-forgiveness.

When you experience these emotions, you have a couple of options. You can surrender to them and drown in your sorrow, guilt, shame, and the mess you have created. Alternatively, you can use these emotions and the accompanying pain to spark change and propel yourself forward.

In the first case, in surrendering and wasting away, you just dig a deeper hole, and create an even greater mess. If you don't take responsibility and instigate change in your life, nothing will improve. Instead, things may constantly worsen, making it ever harder to get back on your feet.

In the second case, where you take responsibility, you

work to undo the damage you have done, and commit in every way to making things right. You learn from your experiences, and you might even inspire others to do the same.

Forgiveness is not a passive process. To forgive yourself, you need to take responsibility and instigate change. If you don't try to make amends for mistakes, it can be hard to forgive yourself. At the very least, you must admit where you were at fault; would you find it easy to forgive another person if they never acknowledged their error?

You might find the mistake was too big to forgive yourself for, but you can still use it to inspire change and start living your life differently. Look for positives which you can take from what you've learned, and find ways to move on, and possibly even derive meaning from it, rather than allowing the incident to rule your life forever.

Take responsibility, make up for your mistakes, and forgive yourself. If you truly messed up, then derive meaning from your experience and allow it to fuel your transformation.

When you start to forgive and accept all parts of yourself, you will discover that you are more capable of doing the same for others, and that you can better understand their struggles. Forgiving yourself for past mistakes can be a blissfully freeing experience, and is essential because you cannot cling to the past if you want to move forward.

Forgiving yourself does not automatically imply that you have done something wrong, just that sometimes your perceptions and expectations convince you that you have.

Forgiveness means looking to the future, instead of becoming fixated on your flaws, regrets, or mistakes.

When it comes to forgiving others, we must understand that we are all different and that our individuality is one of our strengths. An important aspect of forgiveness is having the courage to communicate with and take on the perspectives and individualism of others.

Sometimes when you switch the narrative and try to see the world as the other individual would, their actions become clearer. Even if you cannot reach this sort of understanding, forgive them for your own sake. If you hold on to anger, disappointment, or sadness, that person has taken your peace of mind from you, and they cannot do this unless you allow them to.

Do not let the burden of grudges weigh you down. Remember and learn from experiences, but make peace with them.

Based on Dr. Andrea Brandt from her article in *Psychology Today*[14]:

1. Forgiveness does not entail making excuses for the other person's actions.

2. You do not need to tell the other person that you are forgiving them.

3. It does not mean that you no longer have feelings on the subject or the problems within the relationship.

4. Forgiveness does not mean you must include that person in your life.

5. It is something that you do for yourself not others.

6. Forgiving does not mean forgetting.

Some people associate forgiveness with weakness, but I believe owning up to mistakes and forgiving ourselves is one of our greatest strengths. It allows us to embrace our capacity to learn and grow. Life is about learning, and forgiveness is one of its underestimated tools. After all, it was Mahatma Gandhi who said, *"The weak can never forgive. Forgiveness is the attribute of the strong."*

You need to learn what works and what does not, and to understand what roles you play in any given situation. Noticing your mistakes and filing them in a library in your mind to be forgotten or suppressed is not enough. You need to be able to address them and forgive them so that you can learn from them. If you don't, you will be stuck and unable to experiment with new ways of dealing with your problems.

Most people spend more time and energy going around problems than in trying to solve them.

– Henry Ford

Everything that you forgive sets you free.

To end this chapter on transformation, let's briefly return to our journey analogy. You have booked your trip and you're heading for the plane, but what fuels the journey you're about to take? What makes you keep going when things are difficult? What helped you bolster your courage to fill the emptiness? What motivated you to journey into the depths of yourself to discover the real you?

You have to believe that you are worth the effort, and that you deserve the life you're working toward. You have to love, appreciate, and respect yourself enough to continue down the path of growth, overcome your weaknesses, and show others wholehearted care, love, and appreciation along the way.

Reflection

1. What perceptions do you have to change for transformation to happen? What would you replace them with?

2. What are your current priorities?

3. What should take priority in your transformation: what should you transform first?

4. How can you change old habits into better ones? Which habits would you choose first?

5. If you want to spread your transformation over phases, what would the first phase be?

6. What major obstacles might you encounter as you start your transformation?

7. Is your ideal self realistic yet ambitious?

8. What are you most grateful for in your life?

9. What do you need to forgive yourself and others for so that you are no longer stuck in your current reality?

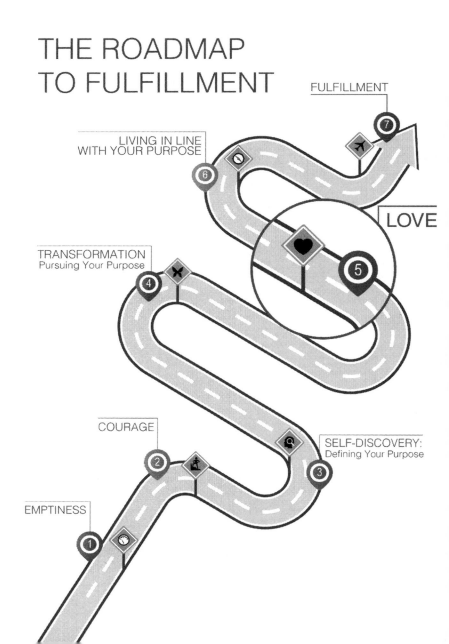

THE ROADMAP TO FULFILLMENT

FULFILLMENT
7

LIVING IN LINE
WITH YOUR PURPOSE
6

LOVE
5

TRANSFORMATION
Pursuing Your Purpose
4

COURAGE
2

SELF-DISCOVERY:
Defining Your Purpose
3

EMPTINESS
1

CHAPTER FIVE
LOVE

God is love.

– John 4:16

You may know Tyler Perry from his film "Diary of a Mad Black Woman." What you may not know, however, is that his life was not always filled with laughter and success. He did not have an easy childhood, and he suffered greatly at the hands of the person who should have been his protector – his father. If his father was displeased with him, his solution was to "beat it out of him."

The only way that he could handle the beatings was

to disassociate himself from what was going on and, as he describes it, to go somewhere else inside his mind. He endured so much throughout his childhood that at the age of 16 it became too much, and he attempted suicide by slashing his wrists.

This was his desperate cry for help as the pressure was mounting and his troubles were persisting. Fortunately, he found solace through writing, which became a form of release. Day after day, he would write letters to himself as a way of reflecting on and processing what had happened to him. After many years, the letters helped him understand the situation better, and gave him the courage to forgive his father for what he had done.

He describes his past as having dragged him down, and frequently impacted his present moment. He was not able to move forward until he forgave his father. He did not do it for his father, but for himself and his well-being. He needed to forgive and move past the hurt.

Using his letters, he created a musical called "I Know I've Been Changed." The musical eventually became famous and opened the door to his writing and directing career. It became an art piece that served as his catharsis and helped him toward forgiveness. Through the letters, he started seeing himself in a better light, and he gained strength and meaning from this experience[1].

Tyler Perry was able to move past an appalling childhood and inspire others to overcome their own obstacles. Only through forgiveness was he able to move forward and love the person he became. This love empowered him to help others.

Love In A Time Of Fulfillment

Love in the model of fulfillment refers to the love, appreciation, and respect we have for the miracle of our being. It is not concerned with selfishness or narcissistic self-love. When used properly, it is one of the strongest forces on Earth, and is absolutely integral to self-motivation, self-inspiration, and growth.

Developing healthy self-love, being fueled by this love, and passing it on to others through service, generosity, creativity and brilliance is a crucial step toward fulfillment. It is, as we mentioned in the last chapter, the fuel of the plane.

Many individuals will pass through their lives, bouncing from one distraction to the next, not taking the time to stop and think about whether changes are necessary, or how to improve themselves. Some of these people do not know that they are worthy of self-love and appreciation. Embarking on the journey toward fulfillment can help give people the boost they need to feel the worth of their being.

Active love is a continuous process which must be present in every stage leading to fulfillment. It allows you to follow your true calling and believe that you are worthy of this exciting adventure, and worthy of living a meaningful life.

According to Dr. Brené Brown, a professor at the University of Houston, the only difference between those who have a strong sense of love and belonging and those who do not is a belief that they are worthy of these qualities[2]. Do you feel worthy of love?

This phase of the process does not necessarily come after the transformation step. In fact, healthy self-love might begin to arise throughout the process, starting in the feeling of emptiness, and continuing through courage, self-discovery, and transformation. Self-appreciation, the belief that you deserve to live a better and more authentic life that is in line with your beautiful true self, is the fuel that powers the entire trip toward fulfillment. The more people love and appreciate themselves, the more they will be motivated to act on their courage and take the plane ride to fulfillment.

Every step that brings you closer to a life of meaning, to an authenticity that discards your masks, increases the opportunities you get to love and appreciate yourself, and consequently share that love with others.

Without self-appreciation and love, you cannot:

- Muster the strength to leave your state of emptiness.

- Summon the courage to look within during self-discovery.

- Summon the courage to transform your life.

- Justify taking emotional risks to rid yourself of dead wood.

- Remain steadfast in the face of difficult and challenging decisions.

- Face your demons without giving up.

- Build your resilience against the waves of resistance you will experience.

- Justify making sacrifices and compromises now for the sake of a better tomorrow.

Self-love is about understanding and appreciating that although you had no hand in your birth – you didn't choose to come into this world – you were graced with life, the most precious gift, and that your greatest responsibility is to take care of that life. Self-love is appreciating the importance of living your life to the fullest. You owe it to yourself, and to the world you joined.

> Loving everything about yourself – even the 'unacceptable' – is an act of personal power. It is the beginning of healing.

– Christiane Northrup

Self-love and appreciation are about accepting the full package of your humanity; that includes your brilliance, your ability to make extraordinary things happen, and the inevitable stumbles in your journey of learning and growth. You must embrace the parts that can be embarrassing, the parts you are less proud of. This type of love acts as a shield from failures and disappointments, giving you the ability to get back up when you fall.

It is vital that this phase fuels your entire journey to

fulfillment, especially transformation, because you will falter while you transform yourself. Those who do not feel worthy may be overwhelmed by their failures, but those who have the anchor of self-love, and the courage that comes with it, will be able to pick themselves up and say, "I'm going to try again, because I deserve another chance, and another, and another..."

Lastly, it is the best way to give love to others. Self-love is essential for being able to give and receive love. If you do not love yourself, or deem yourself worthy of love, the relationships you build will have an insecure foundation. The affection you share in these relationships will not be as strong, and you may not form a lasting connection. A part of you will doubt whether your family or friends love, appreciate, and respect you, because you do not love and appreciate yourself.

Based on Jim Warner's *Facing Pain Embracing Love*, giving and receiving true love is a "two-way experience of sharing grace, compassion, and kindness without measurement or comparison."[3] In order to give love, it must flow through you and replenish you so that you may act as a conduit of love for others.

I want you to imagine the process of giving love as the airline pre-flight safety briefing. The flight attendant informs you that if there is an emergency, you must use your own oxygen mask before helping anyone else with theirs. If you cannot take care of yourself (in this situation, breathe oxygen), then you will not be able to take care of anyone else. Before you go out professing your love to others, love and appreciate yourself. Rollo May put it beautifully: *"Self-love is not only necessary and good, it is a prerequisite for loving others."*

What Is Driving You?

 Service which is rendered without joy helps neither the servant nor the served. But all other pleasures and possessions pale into nothingness before service which is rendered in a spirit of joy.

– *Mahatma Gandhi*

When your actions are driven by insecurities or emotional hungers, you may overlook the places where your help is truly needed. You will put your time and effort into things which quell your own emotional hungers. This may also apply to your relationships.

Some individuals will enter relationships to rid themselves of loneliness, especially if they are surrounded by happy couples. Starting a relationship just for the sake of having a partner will not bring fulfillment. Instead, it will feed an emotional hunger, and when they find that the relationship is not fulfilling their needs, they may move on to other relationships, or jeopardize the relationship they are in. They will search for love and appreciation from others, and forget to turn that love inwards and love and value themselves.

The same thing can apply in a professional context. At times, we may be so driven by the idea of stability and security that we forget what we really want to work on. We replace what we are genuinely interested in and love to do with what we feel stuck doing, making ourselves miserable in the process.

An action that is propelled by self-appreciation is strong and fierce, because the intentions behind the action are genuine. If anything else takes over the steering apparatus, fulfillment may become an illusion. That is why the journey to fulfillment must be driven by healthy self-love and self-appreciation.

When you recognize that you deserve love, you will instinctively begin to respect yourself enough to do what is best for your journey of fulfillment. You will start to identify negative relationships and toxic situations, and you will realize that they are not worth your time. You will also move beyond insecurities and emotional hungers. You will plunge into adventure despite your fears.

It is essential to do this, because you have light and strength within you that are too valuable to waste on negativity. Surround yourself with people and situations that appreciate and nurture your core, and let love be the driving force.

Baggage Claim

Every individual has scars, wounds, and painful experiences. They have parts of their history which weigh more heavily on them than other parts. The importance which individuals assign to events is equivalent to the pain that they felt, and this will differ from person to person. What might seem a trivial occurrence to an outsider may carry great emotional pain for the person who experienced it.

One child could be facing the ultimate pain of not knowing whether or not they will be fed that day. This form of pain is directly related to survival and is terrible. In another home, the child's pain may be due to the fact that they felt their mother did not give them enough attention. Although the first case seems graver, both children can still feel the same amount of pain, because it is based on the child's perception.

We know pain in reference to what we have experienced in life. Two individuals can both feel equal pain in completely different situations. That is why it is important never to judge or compare, for each individual is trying to deal with their own demons.

Know your pains so that you know how to reduce and manage them on your journey, because pain will always be part of life. Pain is distressing, but it also focuses your attention on what needs to be fixed in your life so that you can emerge a more complete person.

You should also know the pains of the other people in your life, because these are part of their story, and key to understanding them and therefore dealing with them in a supportive way.

A life of fulfillment does not mean a life without pain. Every journey carries its own baggage. It is the nature of being.

Our First Love

Our first experience of love comes from our primary caregivers. A child usually forms a strong bond with its mother, and she represents safety, warmth, and protection. A young child always wants their mother nearby. However, if they do not feel that they receive enough love, insecurities start to form. The child will learn how to manipulate their environment to get the attention that they need from their caregiver.

As they grow up, they learn how to behave so that they are "loved," and how to avoid being reprimanded. They begin to adapt and change, to fit the model that best describes the ideal child. Alternatively, if they cannot live up to these expectations, they may go in the opposite direction and rebel.

If the childhood baggage becomes too heavy, some individuals will start to dislike themselves. They will constantly try to prove to their parents and society that they are worthy, but rarely believe it themselves. A young child is dependent on their caregiver for survival, so the actions of the caregiver are crucial in shaping their self-confidence.

In addition to this, the relationship with the caregiver will set the tone for future relationships, especially the relationship with the self.

As you make your journey toward fulfillment and through the phase of self-discovery, issues pertaining to your relationship with your parents are bound to surface. This relationship is one of the bedrocks of your entire psychological structure, and any wounds which remain open will be draining your energy and resources, even if you aren't aware of them.

Unsurprisingly, the best way to heal the wounds of your relationship with your parents is to forgive them and yourself for any pain created on either side of the relationship. You may want to seek a professional to help with this, or you may be able to do it yourself. Forgiving them and moving on will let you focus your energy on growth and fulfillment. You and your parents may still disagree on many things, but you need to make peace and focus on your journey.

Attachment: The One, The Many

There are various forms of attachment that a child can adopt. When a child grows up with a sensitive caregiver who provides a safe and loving home, the child will develop a secure attachment. This secure attachment is crucial to building a strong bond between the child and the caregiver, and it is carried into adulthood[4].

This sort of security is essential to a person's ability to stay calm in times of conflict or panic. If they had a parent present to help them through stress, they will have adopted effective methods for soothing themselves, and they will know that they can cope.

On the other hand, if the caregiver was regularly absent, a child might adopt maladaptive coping strategies and have a much greater sense of fear.

If the child worries that their caregiver will abandon them, they will develop an insecure attachment. They will constantly feel like they have to earn their caregiver's love, appreciation, and respect. This is the breeding ground of insecurities and the hunger to impress others.

It is crucial for an individual to feel lovable and worthy of love. If they do not feel this from their caregivers, it becomes more difficult for them to satisfy the need later in life. People who did not receive love as young children may only be able to experience self-love if they understand that, despite its previous absence, they deserve it.

There is no such thing as a perfect family, but what is crucial is that you focus on fulfillment, and do not allow others to define your value. As a human, it is non-negotiable; you are worthy, unique, capable of correcting your mistakes and learning, and you are lovable.

Don't Forget To Remove The Mask

Love takes off masks that we fear we cannot live without and know we cannot live within.

– *James A. Baldwin*

As mentioned in the self-discovery chapter, to survive people's harsh criticisms and live up to their expectations, individuals will construct an artificial self, which deals with the outside world and adheres to the norms of their society and culture. This is like a mask that each individual learns to wear in order to survive.

> **The reward for conformity is that everyone likes you but yourself.**
>
> *– Rita Mae Brown*

If we wear our masks for too long, we will get stuck with them and forget what our faces look like underneath. The self-discovery and transformation phases help us to remove the masks (at least, many of them), and self-love allows us to have a good relationship with ourselves, making it easier to remove the mask, and grants us the courage to avoid putting the masks back on.

Throughout our lives, people are constantly telling us what we mean to them, ranging from uplifting positive compliments to downright insulting remarks. These comments change how we see ourselves. Our friends might tell us that we are "fun to hang out with," our bosses might complain that we are lazy, or our colleagues might admire our work ethics. All of these remarks slowly start to formulate our overall opinions about who we are.

For instance, many individuals who post pictures of themselves on social media may judge their self-worth based on how many "likes" their pictures receive. If they find that only a few people responded, they may take the lack of "likes" as a testament that they are unlikable, and by extension dislike themselves.

You may have previously placed your sense of self-worth in the hands of others, but it is vital that you do not allow their perceptions of you to fuel your own. You deserve self-appreciation, even if others do not seem to appreciate you. Do not let others be the reason for you to hide behind a mask, and do not let them define your relationship with yourself.

No one can make you feel inferior without your consent.

– Eleanor Roosevelt

Appreciate The Duality Of Our Nature

We all have stories that we are proud to share with others, and we all have stories that we want to hide from the world. We have virtues and vices, angels and demons, and none of us represent one extreme or the other.

To love and appreciate the miracle of our being, we must accept both sides, the beautiful side and the ugly side, the strengths and the weaknesses. We must celebrate both, and accept the existence of the dark.

Past mistakes shouldn't determine whether or not you deserve love and appreciation; and indeed, self-love is what makes you disappointed in the darker sides of your character – because you know that you can do better. If you don't focus on respecting and loving yourself, you may find that the resulting negativity feeds the darker aspects of your character.

When you experience a moment of weakness, or you do something to hurt yourself or others, it is the love and appreciation that you have for yourself and for others that motivates you to make things right. There's nothing wrong with hating your past actions, but never allow that hatred to transfer to yourself. Use self-love to focus on your responsibilities and the best aspects of your character, and appreciate the whole you for everything you are.

Remember that self-love, self-esteem, and self-compassion should not justify dysfunctional attitudes and behavior, and they aren't about settling for a life that is worse than the one you are capable of living. They are about becoming the best you can be, and focusing on the light.

With enough love and appreciation, and through consciousness, responsibility, maturity, meaning, self-discipline, and virtue, you can gradually expand the beautiful aspect of your being, and elevate your life to its fullest potential.

Self-love will help you control your demons, but most will not be dissolved. We must all accept the duality of human nature, and simply focus on the light sides without wasting energy hating or trying to remove the darkness. Through healthy self-love and self-appreciation, we learn to embrace ourselves completely, without exception, and work toward brightening the light within so that we can grow, improve, and share our beauty with others and serve others.

With self-appreciation, you state confidently, "I value my being, even though I hate some of the things that I do. I know I am capable of overcoming my past, dealing with my scars, learning from my mistakes, and avoiding behavior that might cause pain and suffering for me and for others."

This unconditional, positive self-regard does not waver, irrespective of what others say and do. Your own opinion of yourself is what's important – not the opinions of others. It also encourages you to be accountable to yourself, to recognize the emotional scars and hungers, the demons and darkness, and to keep pushing forward to ensure you flourish in life.

Through responsibility, commitment, virtue, discipline, and willpower, you can minimize pain and suffering, tap into your potential, and grow in spite of difficulties.

Self-love encourages you to feel the full spectrum of emotions, to permit yourself grief, anger, and guilt when things go wrong, because you know you can do better. It will ensure that the overriding sensation is one of hope, however, and that you focus on correcting the error and charting the course you want to take.

Love and value yourself in your totality, and focus on

your growth. If you cannot appreciate yourself and your beauty, you are in for a lifetime of worry, unnecessary pain, insecurity, and a misguided, unjust view of the potential greatness that lies within.

Time To Tap Into The Real Lovable You

Don't let the noise of others' opinions drown out your own inner voice.

– Steve Jobs

Focus on tapping into the part of you that is solely controlled by you, not by the opinions of others – the part of your authentic self that is pure, innocent, loving, compassionate, helpful, and beautiful. It strives to be seen and stretch its legs. Without letting this part shine, without loving your authentic self, there will be an obstacle between you and fulfillment.

The irony is that we tend to try and control the outside part of ourselves, which we cannot do because it largely depends on others. The only part of ourselves that we can control is the inner part.

When we try to persuade others to love us, which is something that is outside of our control, we are bound to fail, and we may develop a sense of helplessness. This relates to the concept of *Learned Helplessness*, which was researched by Martin Seligman, renowned positive psychologist and author, following a series of experiments. The main thrust of this notion is that, after a certain amount of failures, individuals begin to believe that their actions have no impact on the outcome, so they lapse into complacency[5].

Recent research, however, suggested that it is not that we learn helplessness, but that we have a biological instinct to conserve energy. If we feel that our actions are futile, we will cease wasting our resources[6]. When we fail to gain other people's love, we may eventually interpret this failure as meaning that we are unworthy of love. If we believe that we are unlovable, the chances that we will be willing to look within (self-discovery) and take initiative to change (transformation) will decrease, preventing us from continuing the journey toward fulfillment.

However, if we learn that we can control our reaction to or perception of a situation – that we can control our authentic self – then we can look within, see that we deserve to experience self-appreciation, and learn to love ourselves.

During self-discovery you are bound to find out a few things about yourself that you don't particularly like. Armed with the belief that you have some semblance of control over your light and dark sides, and a sense of self-love and self-appreciation, you are more likely to be motivated to tap into your authentic self and strive to be the best you can be.

Remember, love in its purest form accepts each individual in their totality, with all their negatives and positives. Love is not about trying to change a person. It is about seeing their light and dark sides and knowing that they are a normal part of being human. The same applies to how you see yourself.

If you do not react well to your own shortcomings, or revel in your strengths, it becomes difficult to do the same for others. If you don't open your eyes to your authentic and lovable self, it becomes a challenge to give and receive love. That is why you must come to terms with your baggage and drop it off. As the famous psychiatrist Carl Jung says, *"Everything that irritates us about others can lead us to an understanding of ourselves."*

For example, imagine that Lucy was a spoiled brat as a child, but eventually learned her behavior was unacceptable. This could make her disdainful of the same behavior in others, because it would remind her of her own struggle and make her feel defensive and angry with herself. Without accepting and addressing her insecurity, Lucy would be unable to find fulfillment and peace.

No one has a perfect childhood; we all have our own scars, emotional hungers, and demons. Despite this, understanding that for all the darkness in our lives there is also light and beauty, might be just what we need to move past them and focus on our worthiness of love. Being human should be celebrated, not considered a weakness. Our ability to overcome challenges makes us beautiful.

Love And Self-Esteem

 As you grow in self-esteem, your face, manner, way of talking and moving will tend naturally to project the pleasure you take in being alive.

– Nathaniel Branden

Our self-esteem directly correlates with how much we appreciate and love ourselves, and how aware we are of the goodness within us. Dr. Abraham Twerski, a psychiatrist and Rabbi, spoke about how he used to struggle with self-esteem and did not even realize it until he went on a vacation to Hot Springs.

It was supposed to be a relaxing and rejuvenating retreat. Part of the treatment included staying in a whirlpool for 25 minutes, sitting in silence and relaxing. After just five minutes, he was already ill at ease, and realized that this unveiled a hidden problem about himself and his own internal struggle. If he was unable to sit alone with his thoughts, this could only mean he did not think well of himself.

This led him on a two-year journey of self-discovery (with the assistance of a fellow psychiatrist), after which he was able to appreciate and accept all parts of himself, to boost his self-esteem and sense of self-worth. There were times when he faltered, of course, but eventually he was able to sit alone with his thoughts and be at peace[7].

Our self-esteem is greatly affected by the stories we tell ourselves. Many people, without realizing it, fall victim to narratives that do not reflect who they truly are. As a result, they end up disliking themselves and suffering from low self-esteem. They do not appreciate themselves enough to experience self-love. Instead they criticize themselves, saying things like, "You are a bad person," "You are no good," "You will never make anything of yourself." These thoughts eventually compound and result in an overall dislike of the self.

The old, false narratives of what you thought of yourself must die, so that a new level of consciousness can be adopted. With love driving your journey, you will succeed in instigating a change and boosting your self-regard.

> Breaking out is following your bliss pattern, quitting the old place, starting your hero journey, following your bliss. You throw off yesterday as the snake sheds its skin.
>
> – *Joseph Campbell*

It is time to ensure that you are embracing who you truly are, loving that person, and nurturing your relationship with yourself. Only then can you build up your self-esteem, realize your self-worth, engage in the true narrative of your life, and learn to appreciate yourself so you may continue your journey of fulfillment.

Do You Love Who You Are?

The question can be difficult to answer with certainty, but if you study your behavior and habits, you will discover clues as to whether you truly love yourself. At times, your distaste for yourself will manifest in the way you treat your body – ignoring your health needs, abusing drugs, and not resting when necessary all indicate a lack of concern for your being. You can also study your inner monologue; do you berate yourself for small failures, and feel irritated with yourself when you're unable to complete a task?

When there is no love of self, you may engage in subconscious self-sabotage. If you are afraid of failing, you will lack faith in your own capabilities, and you may doubt whether you deserve to succeed. These thoughts and feelings control you, and you stand in the way of your own progress.

Think of someone that you love dearly. How do you behave toward this person?

- Do you compliment them, treat them with care, nurture them, and protect them?

- Do you accept the fact that they are not perfect?

- Do you listen to their worries, fears, and doubts? Do you help them overcome these obstacles?

- Do you help lift them up when they are feeling down?

- Do you forgive their mistakes?

- Do you acknowledge their feelings and their right to those feelings?

Use your behavior toward them as a template for how you should behave toward yourself. Treat yourself the same way you would treat someone you are responsible of taking care of. Treat yourself with as much kindness as you would show someone you loved (partner, friend, family member), and remember that they would want you to do this. If you feel frustrated with yourself, step back and re-evaluate how you would respond to a friend making the mistake you have made. If you would comfort them, then don't berate yourself.

Love of others and love of ourselves are not alternatives. On the contrary, an attitude of love towards themselves will be found in all those who are capable of loving others.

– Erich Fromm

If you are capable of loving others, you are capable of loving yourself. It is likely that even in the people you love most dearly, you can see flaws. You love them regardless. Apply this philosophy to your own being. If you can see no other value in yourself, remember that your love for others, despite their fallible nature, is reason enough for you to experience self-love.

Your love for the people you care for and the people
you wish to inspire can give you a reason to love and
appreciate yourself, and can give you a reason to go
through personal transformation.

With enough self-love, you can move past your weaknesses, past the illusion of perfection, and you can allow
failures without being shaken by them; you will use them
to motivate yourself to address them and come out a better
person.

How Do You Open The Door To Love?

Your task is not to seek for love, but merely to seek
and find all the barriers within yourself that you have
built against it.

– *Rumi*

How many times have you heard the phrase, "you
must learn to love yourself"? It's commonly expressed,
but over-simplified and not necessarily helpful. It can take
many years to understand what it means, let alone apply
it. However, it is a starting point, and something you can
return to if you lose your path.

There are practical, conscious decisions you can make when it comes to implementing self-love. You can remind yourself of your greatest triumphs, of your proudest moments, and focus on these achievements when you are struggling with your inner demons.

You can strip away the paralyzing importance you place on your mistakes. Take a different perspective, and – while you must learn from the mistake – give it no more importance than you would give it if a casual acquaintance had made it. Do not allow it to magnify just because it was your mistake, and do not let it overshadow your achievements. Learn to laugh when you do something wrong, make it inconsequential, and move on.

Sometimes mistakes may be too serious to treat lightly. Instead of allowing your shame, regret, and guilt to overwhelm you, use these emotions to motivate you to make up for your mistake, to take responsibility, and to correct the path of your life. Otherwise, you will just surrender to your dark side, and overshadow your beautiful light side in the process.

Remember to be thankful for all that you have and all that you are. Feed your positive perceptions of yourself and your life... feed the love.

Finally, do not allow negativity to distract you from your enjoyment of positivity. Limit the time which you spend analyzing problems and errors, and focus predominantly on finding solutions, on what you enjoy, on your responsibilities and calling, and above all, on the fact that you are alive and capable.

The Five Languages Of Love

Gary Chapman, in his book *The Five Languages of Love*, discusses the five different ways that individuals show and express their love for others. Joyce Marter adapted these same five ways to the self; use them to boost your feelings of love for yourself[8].

The first one is **"words of affirmation."** Use self-encouraging statements to help yourself overcome the challenges you face. Say things like, "I can overcome my difficulties," "I am resilient," "I am strong," "I can do this!" "If others can do it, so can I," "The same way I overcame difficulties in the past, I can overcome these difficulties as well," Believe in yourself, your capabilities and the power that life has given you.

The second is **quality time**. Remember to take the time to meditate or reflect. This is essential, yet challenging, because you must distance yourself from everyday distractions and commitments. Ensure that, even with a busy schedule, you make space for your own needs and wants, for your internal thoughts to take shape and exist. If you don't make room for your being, you cannot energize and love it, because it is lost in the tumult of busyness.

The third language is **physical touch**, which can be done by giving and receiving hugs, getting a massage, stretching, and pampering your body. Listen to your physicality, recognize it, and respond to its needs.

The fourth is **acts of service** – doing things that help you. This means paying attention to the foods you eat, remembering to exercise, spending time with loved ones, and napping if you feel tired. Taking care of yourself is the surest way to feel better; prioritize this wherever possible.

Lastly, **gifts.** Every now and then, it is nice to treat yourself to good things. Pamper yourself with new clothes, new shoes, a new phone, or a well-deserved vacation. This is not about becoming materialistic or expecting happiness to come from objects, but about acknowledging your harmless desires and responding to them. Be kind to yourself.

You Are A Miracle

Remind yourself that being human is, in itself, miraculous. Each individual came into existence despite the odds, and you are no exception. Only one combination out of the nearly infinite number of possibilities could have made you. Accept that this alone makes you extraordinary.

We have barely begun to discover the power and brilliance of human nature and the mind. Can you imagine the incredible possibilities our species represents? Can you find it in yourself to love not just who you are, but the miracle that is you?

Remember that you are unique. The fact that you are the only you that has ever existed, and will ever exist, is a miracle in and of itself. You alone have the potential to use your uniqueness to find fulfillment and to elevate the lives of those around you. This makes you extraordinary — you are one of a kind.

Don't you think it is time to embrace the miracle that you are? It is time that you learn to love yourself, be self-compassionate, embrace your uniqueness, take full responsibility for your being, and let these things fuel your journey of fulfillment.

At this point in the journey, you have chosen your destination, bought your ticket, the plane is fully fueled, and you have just taken off. The take-off may have been turbulent, perhaps exhilarating and nerve-wracking, but now you are in the sky, tracking out a new course on a journey you have chosen.

Reflection

1. How do you feel about yourself?
2. What do you most appreciate about yourself?
3. What do you least appreciate about yourself?
4. Is there anything in your life that you hate yourself for? How is that affecting your life? How can you overcome this feeling and move forward?
5. Imagine someone you are responsible of taking care of:
   - How would you celebrate their beauty and goodness? How would you encourage them to manifest this beauty and goodness even more?
   - How would you encourage them to overcome their dark side and elevate their being? What practical steps would you take to do this?

   Now apply these to yourself and take care of yourself wholeheartedly.
6. How can you forgive yourself for your mistakes and commit to never repeating them?
7. What makes you think you deserve a better life? How can you cherish these qualities more?
8. How can you encourage your commitment to become all that you can become?
9. Do you believe that you owe it to yourself to best that you can be? Why?
10. Do you believe that you owe it to those whom you adore to be all you can be? Why?

THE ROADMAP
TO FULFILLMENT

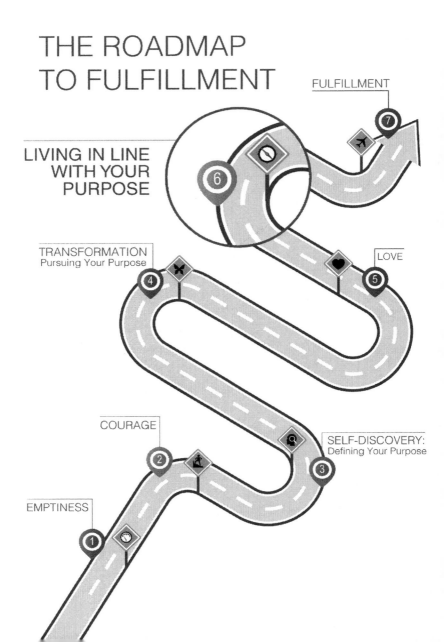

FULFILLMENT

LIVING IN LINE
WITH YOUR
PURPOSE

TRANSFORMATION
Pursuing Your Purpose

LOVE

COURAGE

SELF-DISCOVERY:
Defining Your Purpose

EMPTINESS

CHAPTER SIX
LIVING IN LINE WITH YOUR PURPOSE

> **The good life is a process, not a state of being... It is a direction not a destination.**

– Carl Rogers

She takes 22 pills daily. About 15 years ago, she was diagnosed with a rare disease that affects both her kidneys, and she was not given many years to live. This disease eventually resulted in other complications and led to numerous surgeries. She was also diagnosed with breast cancer and underwent treatment. Despite the many trials that she faced throughout her life, she remained the model of resilience and strength. Even when she was a child, she knew what she wanted to become – a teacher. All her actions reflected her desire to teach and nurture others.

She was unable to have children of her own, but she became a mother-figure to the hundreds of boys and girls she taught over the years. Many of them, who have become parents and accomplished professionals, still visit her to this day, thanks to the lasting impact that she had on their lives and perspectives.

In her family, she serves as the glue, keeping people close, mending fractures, ensuring that the segments remain whole. She is constantly there for others. She takes on everyone's problems without complaining or feeling resentment. She is an extremely positive person and, although life has tested her more than most, she continues to emit strength, stamina, optimism, and energy.

This person is someone I know, cherish, and admire. Individuals like her, who represent strength and courage, who fill their lives with joy in spite of hardships, pain, and suffering, make you proud of being human.

Living your purpose will give you a sense of meaning and fulfillment. At this stage in the journey, you are finally living with the changes that you made during your transformation. All the decisions made and the tickets bought led to this moment. It is time that you embrace it and live a meaningful and purposeful life.

Time To Share

> Each of us carries a unique spark of the divine, and each of us is also an inseparable part of the web of life.

– Viktor E. Frankl

Living in line with your purpose is about sharing your gifts – the best parts of you (your uniqueness) – with the world to benefit and elevate those around you. At this stage, it is time to give back, to share the knowledge that you have gained from this long journey, so that you can live a fulfilled life and motivate and help others start their own journeys.

Remember that in our interconnected world, helping others and contributing to society is not just a form of charity, but a mutually beneficial endeavor – for the more you give, the more you shall receive. This will help heal your own wounds and pains, and help you transcend to fulfillment.

Your uniqueness doesn't have to come from your successes. It can also come from the failures that taught you remarkable lessons which you can share.

What Does It Look Like To Live Purposefully?

The heart is a metaphor for feelings. The soul is a metaphor for who we are at our core, the combination of our conscious and subconscious beings.

Following Your Heart

Imagine knowing deep down that no matter what you are doing, if it is driven by an honorable meaning, it will be right. Living in line with your purpose is when you let this knowledge and sensation guide your every action.

You can count on life being unpredictable and things changing abruptly. You will be prepared for this, because when you live in line with your purpose, you will have structure, meaning, and focus. Decisions will become clearer and you will no longer worry about what you are doing with your life. You will gain a sense of clarity and have clear priorities to guide you, even when you feel uncertainty.

Hard work will no longer feel as hard because you will derive meaning from it. You will love what you are doing, and it will fill you with a sense of achievement. You will be living in the moment, existing in your truest form, focused on offering the world the best that you have.

Your life will be filled with meaning because you are living the most authentic version of yourself, one filled

194

with love and all its derivatives (compassion, care, etc.). When you are filling your days with the things that you truly love, that make you come alive, you are in a state of living your purpose.

You will not wait around for people to reassure you about what you are doing. Their comments, beneficial or otherwise, will not affect you as they may have done previously, because you won't depend on the approval of others. You will follow your purpose because of the peace and meaning it brings you, not so that you can receive love and gratitude from others. It is in this stage that you truly elevate and enhance your life, as well as the lives of others.

If you can tune into your purpose and really align with it, setting goals so that your vision is an expression of that purpose, then life flows much more easily.

– Jack Canfield

Following Your Soul

The purpose of purpose is to provide meaning. Sometimes we derive meaning from pain, suffering, tragedy, and the challenges of life, and sometimes from passions and interests.

We all have duties and responsibilities. Life sometimes throws us onto paths we didn't choose. However, we must find it in ourselves to adapt and flourish in spite of this unexpected change. In many cases, the paths we find ourselves on are fraught with pain and hardship. Many of us would choose different roads if asked, but this is the nature of life. We can either surrender and live empty, shallow lives, or we can embrace self-love, self-appreciation, responsibility and duty, and transform, adapt, and derive meaning from the journey.

Countless people have suffered unexpected hardships, and yet when we look at their lives, we often feel admiration rather than pity. Those who have used their tragedies to springboard themselves forward inspire and awe us with their efforts.

Think about the civil rights activists who were often robbed of their rights, and how these experiences and difficulties helped give them a meaningful purpose to make a difference. There are many examples of people who take pain and suffering – sometimes their own and sometimes others' – and turn it into something beautiful.

Think of volunteers who help refugees, victims of domestic violence, those suffering trauma, etc. They are choosing to immerse themselves in sorrow and pain in order to serve others and make their lives meaningful. They feel a sense of duty and responsibility, sometimes to complete strangers, and they fulfill this.

> In some ways suffering ceases to be suffering at the moment it finds a meaning, such as the meaning of a sacrifice.

– Viktor E. Frankl

Personally, I know of more than one couple who willingly sacrificed and compromised their careers and what they loved to do for the sake of a disabled son or daughter, because this unfortunate twist of fate gave them more meaning and spoke to their very souls. They stepped up and took responsibility. Their child became their ultimate priority. Nothing else could give them this profound sense of meaning.

Remember, much of life is difficult and painful, but in spite of this, we can rise from the ashes and help others do the same, and find meaning that will bring profound peace to our souls.

Heart & Soul As One

Meaning doesn't need to come from one source or another. There are examples in life, and throughout this book, where purpose is the product of both the heart and the soul. Think about the athlete we mentioned earlier on in this book. As a result of his accident, he was able to find purpose and meaning by helping others who experienced tragedies similar to his.

On the same note, it was Tyler Perry's difficult childhood which led him to find solace in writing, and drove him to inspire others who might find themselves in similar situations.

If you derive meaning from your life's circumstances and you are able to define your purpose so that it brings joy to both your heart and soul, that's wonderful!

Following your passion can fill your heart with joy. Following your sense of duty and responsibility can fill your being with peace.

Heart And Soul Out Of Sync

There are times when what we love and what we are responsible for are not the same thing. Sometimes, when our hearts and souls are not in sync, we need to choose to follow our souls (what we have to do) rather than our hearts (what we are passionate about).

Purpose may require us to sacrifice what we love to do for the sake of what we have to do. Our duties and responsibilities are often more meaningful to us than what we are passionate about.

Choosing to follow your heart will give you joy. However, you might risk experiencing a sense of emptiness, guilt, or shame for abandoning your duties toward something that means the world to you, just so that you can follow your heart. In such cases, you may only find true fulfillment if your soul is fed, even if it means sacrificing what you love to do for what you have to do.

The Three Factors Of A Purposeful Life

To live a purposeful and meaningful life, you must have intention, attention, and intensity.

Intention refers to your focus. At this stage, it should be clear to you what your intention is (living in line with your purpose), so use it as your guide for decision-making. If you were the lighting director in a theater, what would your intention be? To light the stage in a way that highlights the action. Nothing purposeful is accomplished without a clear intention.

The next step is **attention**. The best way to master something is to pay full attention to it. We are not built to multi-task, and we can lose focus and direction if we try. The tasks will usually take longer to complete and the quality of our work may suffer. To live a purposeful and meaningful life, you must define your purpose and focus all your attention and resources on it. Returning to the example of the theater, think of attention as determining which part of the stage needs to be lit. What is important? What are your priorities?

Last comes **intensity.** In terms of the spotlight, intensity determines how bright your light will be, how clearly your audience must see your subject, and for how long the spotlight should be focused on a specific part of the stage. No one has ever mastered anything without committing their time and energy to it. You need to hone your strengths with practice and dedication.

When you are living with your purpose, every action is driven by the meaning it provides, and you focus intently on fulfilling it. For example, my purpose is *"to increase global awareness about purpose-driven leadership for a better life for all on the planet,"* and all my actions must adhere to this. The way I communicate with others, my daily routines, and my decision-making – everything I do is meant to serve my purpose.

Let's look at another example: Maryam Mirzakhani. She was born with a natural talent for mathematics. She was able to understand it in ways that few others could even begin to fathom. It flowed through her, and she loved it. She became a professor at Stanford University, and continued her research in the field, inspiring not only other mathematicians, but also women in general, as she was the first woman to win the Field's Medal, which is the most prestigious award in the field of mathematics[1].

She was a symbol of what following your purpose meant, and although she has passed away, the example she has set will continue to inspire others. She loved numbers and mathematical equations. They were her niche; they helped her make sense of the world. Mathematics was the field that she devoted her time to because she knew she could make a real contribution. It shone a light on the best sides of her.

No matter what it is that you have to offer, embrace your uniqueness, and share it with the world. With time, you may inspire others to do the same. Living in line with your purpose allows you to be a beacon of hope for those around you. Let your purpose guide your every action; you never know what difference you might make in the world, or in someone else's life.

Less Time, More Things Done

> Life is not easy for any of us. But what of that? We must have perseverance and, above all, confidence in ourselves. We must believe that we are gifted for something, and that this thing, at whatever cost, must be attained.

– *Marie Curie*

There are always going to be tough times ahead, but when you are living in line with your purpose, you will feel as though the North Star is guiding your way. You will find your efficiency increasing, and your days will become streamlined for a number of reasons.

You will become less reactive and more responsive. You will be focusing on your overall journey, rather than on heat-of-the-moment decisions where you react according to your fluctuating and fleeting emotions.

Undergoing transformation changes your way of thinking. It increases your patience with everyone, including yourself. You will be able to process situations before you act, asking crucial questions: Is this action in line with my purpose? Does this give my life a sense of meaning? Does this bring peace to my soul? You won't allow your instinctive reactions to control you, but will offer a calm response which adheres to your purpose.

Many negative emotions do not generate considered responses, but snap reactions. A person who is in a state of responsiveness understands that for every action they take, there are three different choices: they can act in a way that gets the situation moving forward, they can refrain from doing anything, or they can react impulsively, making matters more complicated.

Living in line with your purpose means that you don't have time to ruminate about the past. Rumination occurs when you live in a state of emptiness. Once you have defined your purpose, you will not waste time on things that do not matter, because your mind will be geared toward your purpose and doing what gives you meaning.

Living in line with your purpose simplifies your decisions. It will become crystal clear what you need to dismiss and what you need to focus on, so you will spend less time feeling confused or indecisive. You will become more flexible about your approach to problems, able to see the bigger picture. You will be able to ensure that the outcome falls within the parameters of your purpose.

Living in line with your purpose eases your internal struggles. With the clarity that this phase offers you, you will no longer feel suffocated by your burdens, fears, insecurities, etc. The struggle within you will have subsided, and although doubts may creep into your mind occasionally, you will be able to quash them with more ease. You will feel a level of confidence in your decisions that will allow you to withstand the waves of negative emotions and uncertainty.

You will no longer take unnecessary risks, but will make adaptive choices that have meaning and direction, ensuring that you don't stray from the path as often as you may have done previously.

It's safe to say that a life that is lived aligned with your purpose saves time, and motivates you to make time for what matters.

Mastery Is Key

Let us return to the concept of intensity and consider it in more depth. At this stage, you are all in, for when you are living in line with your purpose, there is no such thing as halfway.

Your commitment to your purpose can best be maintained if you practice your craft daily, shoulder your responsibilities and attend to your duties, pouring all your heart and soul into what you do.

There are people who mistakenly believe they have found their purpose, but when they try and live by it, they realize that it is harder than they expected and abandon it. Some are excited by the thought of a new endeavor, but once they reach a plateau in their progress, or face an obstacle or some kind of glitch or failure, they lose all their motivation.

The problem is that most people want fulfillment because (even subconsciously) their soul is yearning for it, but they are not committed to their purpose and do not focus on the actual journey, which is just as important. They don't derive a sense of true meaning from their purpose.

When you immerse yourself completely in what you are doing, you make small steps toward your authentic, better self, and you improve your craft. Each day you work toward your purpose increases your authenticity, sense of meaning, and fulfillment, and you should take pride in your progress.

The Beauty Behind Purpose

Purpose is never ending. It is not restricted to labels and roles. If your purpose is to capture life's beautiful moments through a camera lens, this does not end if you are no longer employed as a photographer.

The key is to remain adaptive. If one door closes, open another. For example, I knew a chef who loved his craft so much that he continued to cook meals for the needy even after he had retired. He believed in changing lives through his cooking. A full stomach, after all, equals a happy heart.

Do not limit your purpose to one specific role, because you may miss out on many other ways you can offer your uniqueness to the world. Purpose is limitless; that is the beauty behind it. Get creative and fulfill your purpose with all your being.

An Example Of Living In Line With Your Purpose

Before Oprah Winfrey was the person we know today, she stumbled her way through almost insurmountable hardships, failures, disappointments, and heartbreaking tribulations.

Her childhood was not easy, as her parents were young and separated when she was born. For the first part of her life, she lived with her grandmother on a farm. At one point she was so poor that she had to wear potato sacks instead of clothing. When her grandmother passed away, she moved in with her mother. At the age of 9, she was raped, and had already suffered many counts of sexual and physical abuse[2].

She caught a break at the age of 14, when she was able to escape her terrible childhood and move in with her father. She finally had a stable environment that included discipline and structure. This was her chance to thrive, and thrive she did. At school, she was known for her exceptional grades and magnetic personality.

One of the things she particularly excelled at was speech-making; her engagement and energy drew people to listen to her, and she was passionate about talking to others. At the age of 12, even before she had found stability at home, she was paid to make speeches, and it seems fair to say that she had found her niche.

She became the first black female news anchor at the age of 19. However, her first job experience was not positive. She was humiliated, sexually harassed, and eventually fired seven and a half months later. Fortunately, she knew what her purpose was, so she kept pushing through, and transformed the lowest-rated talk show in Chicago into the highest-rated rate one — "The Oprah Winfrey Show."[3] Compare who she is now to the terrors and miseries of her childhood.

Living your purpose helps to heal the wounds of the past because when you generously and passionately give people the best that you have to offer, they will pay you back with respect, appreciation, and love, which helps your pains and scars fade away. Oprah was able to rise above her suffering and hurt to become the person she wanted to be – fulfilled with being her true self. She embraced her calling, found meaning in her life, and triumphed over many trials.

Open your eyes to the beauty around you, open your mind to the wonders of life, open your heart to those who love you, and always be true to yourself.

– *Maya Angelou*

THE ROADMAP TO FULFILLMENT

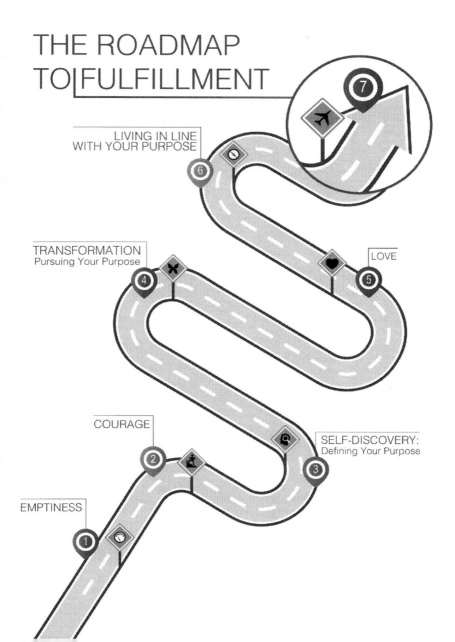

LIVING IN LINE
WITH YOUR PURPOSE

TRANSFORMATION
Pursuing Your Purpose

LOVE

COURAGE

SELF-DISCOVERY:
Defining Your Purpose

EMPTINESS

CHAPTER SEVEN
FULFILLMENT

> **Once an individual's search for meaning is successful, it not only renders him happy but also gives him the capability to cope with suffering.**
>
> *– Viktor E. Frankl*

What do you need to have a full life? What does that mean to you?

To give you insight into my interpretation of fulfillment, let me share a few fragments of my own story with you.

My childhood was not wonderful. I grew up in a country ravished by war. The only certainty was uncertainty.

The main thing we focused on was survival. I had two goals for myself: stay alive and continue my education. I cannot tell you how many days I was almost certain I wouldn't see another dawn.

In my youth, it was normal for my whole family to be huddled in the corridor of our apartment, petrified that a single bombshell could end our little world. I can say that I suffered through some of the darkest moments of my life at that time.

The overall situation left me feeling helpless and worthless. It was as though my life was less valuable than that of a cockroach. For me, the war had no meaning. What was everyone fighting for? The choices of a few warlords left millions scared, confused, displaced, or dead. It made me feel as if human dignity was nonexistent.

One day during the war, my mother's friend visited. During the visit, I remember the sudden rattle of gunfire and the deafening burst of artillery shells falling in our neighborhood. They shook the very foundation of our building, and set the woman trembling, with all the blood drained from her face. She was gripped with fear. She wanted to escape, to run, to hide.

That was how we all looked and felt. Often, when I stepped outside and went to university, I was not sure if I would be coming back. This whole period of my life was not marked by fulfillment, but by fear (it could even be called "fulfearment!").

This, of course, wasn't my story alone. Millions of people who lived in wars have more chilling stories to tell.

I lost all my close friends during the war. My best friend was impaled by an ax, and his heart was ripped right out of his chest. Another friend's body was destroyed when a suicide truck loaded with a ton and a half of explosives blew next to his car. I spent days collecting what was left of him in a small plastic bag. There wasn't enough for us to give him a proper burial, so we only used a photograph at his funeral.

The state of fear continued, even when I started to work. I got a job at *Reuters* as a journalist. It was probably the last job that I would ever have imagined myself doing.

Nonetheless, it was an exciting one: I was a war correspondent and had to report on aspects of the war that most would be too afraid to fathom. It taught me a lot about what it meant to truly live. Sometimes the fighting got so bad that we would be stuck in the office for days at a time with scanty supplies.

In one month, three of my colleagues were killed, while reporting news from the warzones in the city. Some things in life stay with you, like a recurring nightmare. The death that surrounded me during that time is something I will never shake off.

Despite all of this, I became engrossed in my work, and I enjoyed writing. However, I did not feel fully satisfied. I did not feel that I was being completely myself. I did well as a Reuters war journalist, but I cannot say that I had found my purpose in writing about war and destruction. A few years later, I moved on to other roles within the organization that were focused on management and leadership, and suddenly I felt in my element, in love with my work.

Leadership, management, and the art of mobilizing people, organizations, and countries have always been my passion, and I prospered in that field. At university, the first management book I had was 680 pages, and I read it all before the course even started. By comparison, I found other subjects uninspiring, so you can imagine my excitement when I was promoted to management positions.

I was doing something that I loved to do, and that I was good at. I began to grow and my career skyrocketed, but the negative aspects of an international corporate career and its heavy toll on personal and family life detracted from some of the joy.

Fulfillment happened when I decided to align all aspects of my life with my authentic nature — with what I truly wanted to do. I love leadership. I am passionate about it and about elevating people's awareness of their own lives and the wonders they are capable of as they lead individuals and groups into growth and fulfillment. I want people to be as passionate about leadership as I am, and to see it on a new, deeper level.

For me, leadership's ultimate purpose is mobilizing people to overcome their challenges, capture opportunities, and experience a life of fulfillment and growth. This extends to all personal and professional aspects of their lives, including themselves, their families, their organizations, and their communities.

Fulfillment happened when I decided to leave the corporate world and dedicate my life to a purpose that was authentic to me. I had to make major sacrifices for this, leaving behind the luxury and comfort of being the CEO of a number of organizations, and branching out into the instability of starting my own personal venture. It was only then that I started to experience fulfillment.

It was not easy. There were many ups and downs throughout the process. I was still operating in a world that had an unlimited number of variables over which I had no control, and which threw obstacles in my path wherever I turned. Because I was approaching these obstacles with a sense of fulfillment, however, I was able to summon inner strength, overcome them, and continue on the path I had chosen.

One of the memorable periods in my personal journey was in my self-discovery phase, when I realized that I didn't want to spend my life writing about wars, conflicts, and petty politics. Although I appreciated the job, it did not feel like a true reflection of me.

It was only in the universe of leadership that I started to feel true to myself and now, when I write books, give speeches, and conduct seminars about leadership, I feel invigorated, refreshed, alive – the topic gives me so much energy and vivacity. During the seminars, I benefit as much as any participant, because each one reminds me what it means to act out my full being.

It is important to realize that no matter what might be happening in your life, if you are satisfied with who you are, and you feel that you are working to improve yourself, live your purpose, and help others, then your sense of fulfillment will be unshakable.

Fulfillment is a state where you will feel aligned and in sync with the natural rhythm of life. Like a surfer riding a wave, you will flow with the water, but the nature of the ocean, with all its opportunities and risks, remains the same.

Full, Fill, and Ment

99
Many persons have a wrong idea of what constitutes true happiness. It is not attained through self-gratification, but through fidelity to a worthy purpose.

– Helen Keller

Remember that fulfillment at its core comes from the word "full." Your life will be fueled by a sense of purpose, and it will be filled with meaning and all the qualities and filters that are in line with your purpose and your authentic self.

There are many choices to make in life. You can prioritize comfort, you can allow yourself to suffer unnecessarily, or you can opt for an experience that transcends internal suffering and brings you deep joy and inner peace. When you are truly fulfilled, you will have peace of mind and a passion for life.

Remember, when you are fulfilled, you do not allow your negative emotions to control your mind. Instead you know that such emotions belong to particular situations, and you understand their significance, give them meaning, and overcome them.

Fulfillment allows you to focus on your connections with others and their needs. When you experience a state of fulfillment, you have transcended the self and grown beyond your limits. In doing so, you are like a candle, lighting the way for others, and making the world brighter for everyone, including yourself.

Fulfillment transcends happiness into a state of deep, peaceful, and meaningful existence. It is act of love toward yourself and, through you, to the world.

To further this point, let's look at the fact that Abraham Maslow amended his pyramid of needs to include self-transcendence at the top, instead of self-actualization. In his book *The Farther Reaches of Human Nature*, Maslow describes self-transcendence as follows[1]:

"Transcendence refers to the very highest and most inclusive or holistic levels of human consciousness, behaving and relating, as ends rather than means, to oneself, to significant others, to human beings in general, to other species, to nature, and to the cosmos."

External Rewards Do Not Last

> Fame or integrity: which is more important? Money or happiness: which is more valuable? Success or failure: which is more destructive? If you look to others for fulfillment, you will never truly be fulfilled. If your happiness depends on money, you will never be happy with yourself. Be content with what you have; rejoice in the way things are. When you realize there is nothing lacking, the whole world belongs to you.
>
> *– Lao Tzu*

Many individuals define fulfillment based on things outside of themselves. For example, they may mistake fulfillment for being rich or famous. Although such things can potentially make your life easier, they only offer short-term peace of mind and do not lead to fulfillment.

One day, two of my colleagues were discussing what would make them fulfilled. One of them used the analogy of a table. They said that there are four legs to a table and when they are all strong, the table is sturdy. According to my colleague, the four legs were, 1) family, 2) social life and friends, 3) work, and 4) love in the form of finding someone to share your life with.

As I listened to their conversation, the first thought that popped into my mind was that all these elements were external. Many individuals today regard "happiness" or "fulfillment" as being dependent on external factors, things that we have no control over. Although their analogy did mention aspects of our lives that are important, which some may argue are essential components of a "happy life," depending on things that are subject to change will be more likely to grant you temporary "happiness" and make you more vulnerable.

Take some time to consider the model of fulfillment based on my colleague's table analogy.

- What if you lose a member of your family?
- What if you never find the love of your life?
- What if you and a friend drift apart?
- What if you get fired from your job?

If you base your fulfillment on things that are external, you will live a life filled with major ups and downs, because here is the hard truth: the outside world will seldom be the way you want it to be. When things on the outside work out well, they may boost your fulfillment on the inside, but temporarily, giving you fleeting "happiness."

Things that are outside of yourself have diminishing returns – they lose their value over time. For instance, when you listen to a song you like for the first time, the experience is wonderful. After you have listened to it repeatedly, the original excitement begins to fade away. Even relationships become less exhilarating as time passes, though the love may remain undiminished.

External elements and forces are important because we live in a context, not in a vacuum, but if our lives are centered around our external environments, and what anchors us or gives us meaning is outside of ourselves, we will become empty when those elements are removed.

If your anchor or meaning is within you, you become buoyant and resistant to external factors – a key aspect of fulfillment.

Certain governments, such as the United Arab Emirates, have created governmental entities and appointed a Minister who is responsible for "happiness."[2] The country of Bhutan even seeks to measure Gross National Happiness over Gross National Product[3]. Although such initiatives are to be commended, we must not forget the importance of individual autonomy. There is only so much a government can do in order to help individuals attain happiness, or as we have redefined it, fulfillment.

The government can provide its citizens with the essentials, such as safety and an environment conducive to economic growth and creativity, so that individuals have a space to actualize themselves and reach their full potential, but fulfillment is a personal journey. Providing space for people to realize their true potential is crucial, but each individual must also seize the initiative and take responsibility for their own fulfillment.

Fulfillment Is A Lifestyle

> How do you find the divine power in yourself? The
> word enthusiasm means 'filled with a god,' that's
> what it means. So what makes you enthusiastic?
> Follow it . . . So I have a little word: follow your bliss.
> The bliss is the message of God to yourself. That's
> where your life is.

– Joseph Campbell

Bear in mind that fulfillment is not just about happiness. It is not just about authentic living. It is not just about well-being. Fulfillment is about all of these things. It is a much deeper state of being that is driven by the need to derive and be guided by meaning, responsibility, maturity, and striving to become all that you are capable of becoming.

It is about discovering what makes your heart sing and your soul soar, and using it to elevate your life and the lives of others. When you see how this inspires and connects you to others, fulfillment will come naturally, and you will live wholeheartedly.

When you experience fulfillment, you fully and readily accept who you are, and you strive to embody the complete person that you can become. You celebrate the reality that you are in, and in every instance of your life, you are present and engaged. You do not allow emotions to take control or overwhelm you. You no longer chase happiness, but embrace the wide spectrum of emotions. You live realistically and authentically.

You may stumble, making mistakes along the way, but you embrace them, learn from them, and continue on your journey. You may experience pain, but you look at these experiences as a way to grow. Fulfillment fuels your commitment to a purposeful, meaningful, and authentic life.

Based on Jim Warner's book, authentic living means to "love what is," which means we fully accept things as they are[4].

An individual that is living authentically is not afraid to take full responsibility for their life. They do not point fingers when problems arise. They understand their contribution to difficulties and try and solve them. They are open and honest, discarding their masks, and unafraid of the opinion of others.

They are prepared for highs and lows, and focus on the things that they have, as opposed to what is missing in their lives. When new opportunities arise, they are keen to receive them. They do not care to always be right, but to always be learning. Someone who lives an authentic life is caring and compassionate, and forgiving of themselves and others, yet fully understands their responsibilities and duties, and appreciates the consequences of their actions.

All of these aspects may seem overwhelming. You do not have to fulfill all of these states to authentically live, but you can strive for them, especially transparency and openness. Fulfillment is about appreciating your core need for growth.

Remember, humans strive toward purposeful and meaningful growth. At first we grow physically, and then emotionally, socially, intellectually, and spiritually. As we gather more information that contributes to our awareness, we become better equipped to battle our demons. The more we battle the demons within, the more we grow and the stronger we become.

Fulfillment does not promise happiness. It does not mean life will be easy, free of pain and suffering. It does not mean that all your problems will be over, and you can live on cruise control. It is not free of worry and anxiety.

Fulfillment is a state where bearing the hardships of life will be justified and embraced with internal peace. It is a state where the purpose of life is experienced as a living reality. It is a state where you understand and experience your reason for being.

Fulfillment is when you know that, deep down, you are alive!

Welcome To Fulfillment

Of course, happiness is very important. Who wants to spend their lives feeling sad? No one. However, happiness is a feeling, just like fear, loneliness, anger, regret, excitement, compassion, guilt, frustration, etc.

When we say we want to live for happiness, what happens to the other feelings that make us human?

If you lose one of your family members, what do you say to yourself? "I want to be happy"?

If your friend's mother dies, what do you tell yourself and tell her, "let's be happy"?

If your partner betrays you, would you be "happy"?

If you are going through tough times and are overwhelmed and in despair, could you still feel "happy"?

Are you "happy" when you hear stories of injustice, poverty, tyranny, malevolence, abuse, and so on?

Life is painful, but it is also beautiful and joyful.

So, how do we solve the contradiction of wanting to be happy and the existence of pain which is a natural part of life? We cannot avoid the pain, but if we're constantly seeking happiness, this means that – at least some of the time – we must fail to find it. We cannot be happy when loved ones die or terrible tragedies occur, and that means that these moments are associated with failure as well as all the other negative emotions. Life is too complex to make happiness supersede all other emotions and priorities.

Happiness is only as essential to our lives as the other emotions. They all play a fundamental role in living a healthy personal, social, and professional life. We will face days when sadness plays its part, and days when happiness does. We will contend with storms and blissful days on the beach – we might even face the odd tsunami.

Happiness cannot be our compass through all of life's events. It has its place and it is important, but it is not everything. We must find something more substantial and deeper to dedicate our energy to.

So what do we do?

- We accept the reality of life and the fact that our greatest challenge is to survive and grow in spite of obstacles. In this context, it would be childish to make happiness the ultimate goal of life.

- We carry our scars and the baggage of life with responsibility, strength, honor, and grace.

- We make fulfillment our goal so that we can live life to the fullest, with all that it entails – all the challenges and pain and joys and triumphs. What could be better than living an authentic life and making the best out of the years that we have on this beautiful blue planet?

By accepting the reality of life, intelligently dealing with it, and making the best of it, we can complete the greatest adventure we will ever embark on: the adventure of living authentically and truthfully in the fullest possible way.

Unless we live authentically with ourselves and others, unless we live a life that is full of reality, truth, meaning and responsibility, we may be physically alive but our souls – the cores of our beings – will be buried in superficiality, impulsiveness, and restlessness.

If life is a painting, fulfillment is the courage to discover the colors of our souls and elegantly integrate these with life's color palette, so that the painting of life, which we are part of, becomes more beautiful for everybody.

Fulfillment happens when we decide that life is worth living. We need to summon all our courage to look within and see who we truly are. We will then see how to make this discovery of ourselves manifest itself into a state of being with truthfulness, meaning, and responsibility.

Will this be easy? Of course not. It is never easy to stay afloat in troubled waters, let alone when diving into the depth of being – but what is the alternative? To live in the shallowness of a superficial life, or to stay on the surface being tossed around by changing winds and rough waves? Living in emptiness is living in restlessness, in a state of constant crisis, trying not to drown.

It's time to make the decision, the most important decision of your life, to move from living on the surface to living all in, diving deep into the ocean and enjoying the richness and treasures that it offers.

If you are able to do this, you may say before you die, "I lived a full life. Every part of my being was intensely alive. While I was at it, I made life a little better, at least for the people around me, and maybe even for strangers. It made me matter and made my life a story worth remembering and telling."

You are on the plane, looking out of the window, and you are seeing new horizons. It is beautiful... it's very beautiful.

You're alive. Start living!

What else is there to do?

Fulfillment

NOTES

Why This Book

1. Pratt, Laura A., et al. "Antidepressant Use in Persons Aged 12 and Over: United States, 2005–2008." *NCHS Data Brief.* National Center for Health Statistics, no. 76, Oct. 2011.

2. Fisher, Richard. "Future - Why the Present Day Could Be the Best Time to Be Alive." *BBC News,* BBC, 28 Sept. 2016, www.bbc. com/future/story/20160928-why-the-present-day-could-be-the-best-time-to-be-alive?ocid=twfu.

3. Alberto Villoldo. *One Spirit Medicine: Ancient Ways to Ultimate Wellness.* Hay House, Inc, 2016.

4. Vince, Gaia. "Cities: How Crowded Life Is Changing Us." *BBC Future,* BBC, 17 May 2013, www.bbc.com/future/article/20130516-how-city-life-is-changing-us.

5. SWNS. "Americans Check Their Phones 80 Times a Day: Study." *New York Post,* New York Post, 8 Nov. 2017, nypost. com/2017/11/08/americans-check-their-phones-80-times-a-day-study/.; Naftulin, Julia. "Here's How Many Times We Touch Our Phones Every Day." *Business Insider,* Business Insider, 13 July 2016, www.businessinsider.com/dscout-research-people-touch-cell-phones-2617-times-a-day-2016-7.

6. Feiler, Bruce. "For the Love of Being 'Liked'." *The New York Times*, The New York Times, 20 Dec. 2017, www.nytimes. com/2014/05/11/fashion/for-some-social-media-users-an-anxiety-from-approval-seeking.html.

7. History.com Editors. "Industrial Revolution." *History.com*, A&E Television Networks, 29 Oct. 2009, www.history.com/topics/ industrial-revolution/industrial-revolution.; "The Industrial Revolution and the Changing Face of Britain." *British Museum* - The Industrial Revolution and the Changing Face of Britain Page 3,www.britishmuseum.org/research/publications/online_ research_catalogues/paper_money/paper_money_of_england__ wales/the_industrial_revolution/the_industrial_revolution_3. aspx.; Rafferty, John P. "The Rise of the Machines: Pros and Cons of the Industrial Revolution." *Encyclopædia Britannica*, Encyclopædia Britannica, Inc., www.britannica.com/story/ the-rise-of-the-machines-pros-and-cons-of-the-industrial-revolution.

8. Meyer, Adolphe Erich, and Abdou Moumouni. "Western Education in the 19th Century." *Encyclopædia Britannica*, Encyclopædia Britannica, Inc., 26 June 2019,www.britannica. com/topic/education/Western-education-in-the-19th-century#ref47597.

9. The Open Door Web Site. "Social Development in the Industrial Revolution", *The Open Door Web Site*. www.saburchill.com/ history/chapters/IR/071.html.

10. Rafferty, John P. "The Rise of the Machines: Pros and Cons of the Industrial Revolution." *Encyclopædia Britannica*, Encyclopædia Britannica, Inc., www.britannica.com/story/the-rise-of-the-machines-pros-and-cons-of-the-industrial-revolution.

11. Cellan-Jones, Rory. "Stephen Hawking Warns Artificial Intelligence Could End Mankind." *BBC News*, BBC, 2 Dec. 2014, www.bbc.com/news/technology-30290540.

12. Frey, Carl Benedikt, and Michael A. Osborne. "The Future of Employment: How Susceptible Are Jobs to Computerisation?" *Technological Forecasting and Social Change*, vol. 114, 2017, pp. 254–280., doi:10.1016/j.techfore.2016.08.019.

13. UN DESA Department of Economic and Social Affairs. "World Population Projected to Reach 9.8 Billion in 2050, and 11.2 Billion in 2100", *United Nations,* United Nations. www.un.org/development/desa/en/news/population/world-population-prospects-2017.html.

Introduction

1. Niemiec, Christopher.P. (2014) Eudaimonic Well-Being. In: Michalos A.C. (eds) Encyclopedia of Quality of Life and Well-Being Research. Springer, Dordrecht

2. Steptoe, Andrew et al. "Subjective Wellbeing, Health, and Ageing." *The Lancet*, vol. 385, no. 9968, 14 Feb. 2015, pp. 640–648., doi:10.1016/s0140-6736(13)61489-0.; "Sense of Meaning and Purpose in Life Linked to Longer Lifespan." UCL News, University College London, Gower Street, London, WC1E 6BT, UK, 6 Nov. 2014, www.ucl.ac.uk/news/news-articles/1114/061114-longer-lifespan.

Chapter One

1. Pg. 101 in Viktor E. Frankl. *Man's Search for Meaning*. Beacon Press, 2017.

2. Jim Warner. *Facing Pain - Embracing Love: The Map to Authentic Living*. OnCourse Publishing, 2012.

3. Fournier, Gillian. "Anhedonia | Encyclopedia of Psychology."
   Psych Central, 8 Jan. 2018, psychcentral.com/encyclopedia/
   anhedonia/.; "Anhedonia." *Egyptian Journal of Medical Human
   Genetics,* Elsevier, www.sciencedirect.com/topics/neuroscience/
   anhedonia

4. Skirrow, Paul, and Ewan Perry. *The Maslow Assessment of
   Needs Scales (MANS): An Outcome Measure and Planning
   Tool for People with Intellectual Disabilities.* Mersey Care NHS
   Trust, 2009; "Abraham Maslow" in Collin, Catherine, et al. *The
   psychology book: big ideas simply explained.* DK Publishers, 2012.
   Pp. 138-139.

5. Saiidi, Uptin. "How Social Media Is Making Us Less Social:
   Study." CNBC, CNBC, 19 Oct. 2015, www.cnbc.com/2015/10/15/
   social-media-making-millennials-less-social-study.html.

6. Rosemond, John. "What I Call Vitamin N - 'No' - Can Do
   Wonders for a Child's Well-Being." *Lexington Herald Leader,*
   Lexington Herald Leader, 5 May 2015, www.kentucky.com/
   living/family/article44597919.html. ; Rosemond, John. "John
   Rosemond: Today's Parents Have a 'Vitamin N' Deficiency."
   Omaha.com, Omaha World-Herald, 17 July 2017, www.omaha.
   com/momaha/john-rosemond-today-s-parents-have-a-vitamin-
   n-deficiency/article_02492ad7-ac17-5021-9c2a-2b33b4418054.
   html.

7. "Ramesh Sitaraman's Research Shows How Poor Online Video
   Quality Impacts Viewers." *College of Information and Computer
   Sciences,* 11 Feb. 2013, www.cics.umass.edu/news/latest-news/
   research-online-videos.

8. Pg.86 in Viktor E. Frankl. *Man's Search for Meaning.* Beacon
   Press, 2017.

9. A psychological term used to describe members of the research
   team who disguise themselves as participants in the experiment.

10. McLeod, Saul. "Asch Experiment." *Simply Psychology,* Simply Psychology, 2008, www.simplypsychology.org/asch-conformity. html.; "Solomon Asch" in Collin, Catherine, et al. *The psychology book: big ideas simply explained.* DK Publishers, 2012. Pp. 224-227.

11. Oaklander, Mandy. "Tylenol and Acetaminophen: Can Painkillers Ease Emotional Pain?" *Time,* Time, 17 Apr. 2015, time.com/3825042/tylenol-emotion-acetaminophen/; "Broken Hearts Really Hurt." *Association for Psychological Science,* 21 Feb. 2012, www.psychologicalscience.org/news/releases/broken-hearts-really-hurt.html.

12. This is a famous phrase associated with the movie "Forrest Gump". *Forrest Gump.* Directed by Robert Zemeckis. Paramount Pictures, 6 Jul 1994.

Chapter Two

1. Goodyear, Dana. "The Magus." *The New Yorker,* The New Yorker, 18 June 2017, https://www.newyorker.com/ magazine/2007/05/07/the-magus.

2. BBC World Service. "Paolo Coelho – The Alchemist." *World Book Club.* December 2004, https://www.bbc.co.uk/ programmes/p02r7gnl.

3. A United States Navy Vice Admiral and aviator awarded the medal of honor

4. Javanbakht, Arash, and Saab, Linda. "What Happens in the Brain When We Feel Fear." *Smithsonian.com,* Smithsonian Institution, 27 Oct. 2017, www.smithsonianmag.com/science-nature/what-happens-brain-feel-fear-180966992/.

5. A personal correspondence between the author and Nelson Mandela during a talk that the late Mandela gave at the American University of Sharjah, in Sharjah, United Arab Emirates.

6. James B. Stockdale. *Courage under Fire: Testing Epictetus's Doctrines in a Laboratory of Human Behavior.* Hoover Institution Press, 1993.

7. Martin E. P. Seligman. *Learned Optimism: How to Change Your Mind and Your Life.* Vintage, 2006.

8. Pg. IV in Alberto Villoldo. *Courageous Dreaming: How Shamans Dream the World into Being.* Hay House, 2008.

9. Alberto Villoldo. *Courageous Dreaming: How Shamans Dream the World into Being.* Hay House, 2008.

Chapter Three

1. This refers to a choice the protagonist makes — to take the red pill — to escape the illusion of the matrix and return to reality. *The Matrix.* Directed by the Wachowskis, *Warner Bros.*, 31 Mar. 1999

2. Stafford, Tom. "Future - Are We Naturally Good or Bad?" *BBC News,* BBC, 14 Jan. 2013, www.bbc.com/future/story/20130114-are-we-naturally-good-or-bad.

3. To help identify the voices and overcome them, look up Michael Kouly. *Mute: The voices that won't shut up... and you may not know are there!.* Michael Kouly, 2018.

4. Jussim, Lee. "Self-Fulfilling Prophecy." *Encyclopædia Britannica,* Encyclopædia Britannica, Inc., www.britannica.com/topic/self-fulfilling-prophecy.

5. Schanberg, S. (1995). The genetic basis for touch effects. In T. Field (Ed.), *Touch and Early Experience* (pp. 67-80). Mahwah, NJ: Erlbaum; Narvaez, Darcia F. "Where Are the Happy Babies?" *Psychology Today,* Sussex Publishers, 28 Aug. 2011, www. psychologytoday.com/us/blog/moral-landscapes/201108/where-are-the-happy-babies.

Chapter Four

1. Burkeman, Oliver. "This Column Will Change Your Life: Self-Perception Theory." *The Guardian*, Guardian News and Media, 5 Oct. 2012, www.theguardian.com/lifeandstyle/2012/oct/05/change-your-life-self-perception-theory.

2. Martin E. P Seligman. *Flourish: A Visionary New Understanding of Happiness and Well-Being.* Free Press, 2013.

3. Wiseman, Richard. "The Luck Factor." *Skeptical Inquirer*, vol. 27, no. 3, 2003.

4. Tal Ben-Shahar. *Being Happy: You Don't Have to Be Perfect to Lead a Richer, Happier Life.* McGraw-Hill, 2011.

5. Ibid.

6. Charles Duhigg . *The Power of Habit: Why We Do What We Do in Life and Business.* Random House Trade Paperbacks, 2014.

7. Nir Eyal. *Hooked: How to Build Habit-Forming Products.* Edited by Ryan Hoover, Portfolio/Penguin, 2014.

8. Joseph Campbell. *Pathways to Bliss: Mythology and Personal Transformation.* Edited by David Kudler, New World Library, 2004

9. Marshall Goldsmith and Mark Reiter. *Triggers.* Crown Business, 2015.

10. J. C. Maxwell, *15 Invaluable Laws of Growth: Live Them and Reach Your Potential.* Center Street, 2014.

11. Joseph Campbell and Bill D. Moyers. *The Power of Myth*. Anchor Books, 1991

12. Jim Warner. *Facing Pain - Embracing Love: The Map to Authentic Living*. OnCourse Publishing, 2012.

13. Biography in "Nick Vujicic." *Nick Vujicic*, www.nickvujicic.com/.

14. Brandt, Andrea. "How Do You Forgive Even When It Feels Impossible? (Part 1)." *Psychology Today*, Sussex Publishers, www. psychologytoday.com/blog/mindful-anger/201409/how-do-you-forgive-even-when-it-feels-impossible-part-1.

Chapter Five

1. Donaldson, Catherine Victoria. "Tyler Perry Biography." *Encyclopedia of World Biography*, www.notablebiographies.com/ newsmakers2/2006-Le-Ra/Perry-Tyler.html.

2. Brown, Brené. *The Power Of Vulnerability*, TED: Ideas Worth Spreading, www.ted.com/talks/brene_brown_on_vulnerability.

3. Jim Warner. *Facing Pain - Embracing Love: The Map to Authentic Living*. OnCourse Publishing, 2012.

4. Shorey, Hal. "The Keys to Rewarding Relationships: Secure Attachment." *Psychology Today*, Sussex Publishers, 12 Feb. 2015, www.psychologytoday.com/us/blog/the-freedom-change/201502/the-keys-rewarding-relationships-secure-attachment.

5. Seligman , Martin E.P. "Learned Helplessness." Annual Review of Medicine, vol. 23, no. 1, 1972, pp. 407–412., doi:10.1146/ annurev.me.23.020172.002203.

6. Maier, Steven F., and Seligman, Martin E. P. . "Learned Helplessness at Fifty: Insights from Neuroscience." *Psychological Review,* vol. 123, no. 4, 2016, pp. 349–367., doi:10.1037/rev0000033.

7. Abraham Twerski. *My Own Struggle with Low Self-Esteem,* Vimeo, 28 Jul. 2008, vimeo.com/3011249.

8. Marter, Joyce. "Self-Love Must Come First: How to Love Yourself." *The Huffington Post,* TheHuffingtonPost.com, 15 Feb. 2017, www.huffingtonpost.com/joyce-marter-/selflove-must-come-first-_b_9237282.html.

Chapter Six

1. Lamb, Evelyn. "Mathematics World Mourns Maryam Mirzakhani, Only Woman to Win Fields Medal." *Scientific American,* 17 July 2017, www.scientificamerican.com/article/mathematics-world-mourns-maryam-mirzakhani-only-woman-to-win-fields-medal/.; Rafi, Kasra. "Maryam Mirzakhani (1977–2017)." *Nature News,* Nature Publishing Group, 6 Sept. 2017, www.nature.com/articles/549032a

2. Harris, Paul. "'You go, girl' The Observer Profile: Oprah Winfrey." *The Guardian,* Guardian News and Media, 20 Nov. 2005, www.theguardian.com/media/2005/nov/20/television.usa.

3. "Oprah Winfrey Biography." *Encyclopedia of World Biography,* www.notablebiographies.com/We-Z/Winfrey-Oprah.html

Chapter Seven

1. Pg. 269 in Abraham H. Maslow. *The Farther Reaches of Human Nature.* Viking Press, 1971.

2. Bayoumy, Yara. "Want to Be Happy, Tolerant, Young? UAE Has a Ministry for That." Edited by Maha El Dahan and Jeremy Gaunt, *Reuters*, Thomson Reuters, 10 Feb. 2016, www.reuters.com/article/us-emirates-government-happiness-idUSKCN0VJ1NW.; Weller, Chris. "The United Arab Emirates Just Appointed Its First Ministers of Happiness and Tolerance." *Business Insider*, Business Insider, 10 Feb. 2016, www.businessinsider.com/united-arab-emirates-appoints-minister-of-happiness-2016-2.

3. Kelly, Annie. "Gross National Happiness in Bhutan: the Big Idea from a Tiny State That Could Change the World." *The Guardian*, Guardian News and Media, 1 Dec. 2012, www.theguardian.com/world/2012/dec/01/bhutan-wealth-happiness-counts.

4. Jim Warner. *Facing Pain - Embracing Love: The Map to Authentic Living*. OnCourse Publishing, 2012.

About The Author

Michael Kouly began his career as a Reuters war journalist. He covered armed conflicts that involved, Israel, Lebanon, Syria, Iran, Hezbullah, Islamic extremists, terrorism, the United States, Kuwait, Iraq and others... He also covered musical concerts, fashion shows and car racing.

Writing about wars, geopolitics, international diplomacy, and global events offered Michael unique opportunities to witness, analyze and write about leadership at the highest levels: where bad leadership meant the loss of thousands of lives and good leadership led to avoiding wars, saving lives and rebuilding shattered countries.

Michael also exercised corporate leadership over a period of 30 years as he led the growth of regional and international businesses. He is a three-time CEO and president at organizations like Reuters, Orbit and Cambridge Insti tute for Global Leadership, managing people in more than 20 countries.

Over the span of his career, Michael made some good decisions that generated remarkable success and also some not so good decisions that offered valuable lessons on what works and what doesn't when exercising leadership - emphasizing the mindset of "you either win or learn".

From as far back as he can remember, Michael has been fascinated by leadership. He has spent his life learning about leadership, purpose and strategy by practicing them, watching others lead and by conducting extensive research on the art and science of mobilizing people and organizations towards growth and noble purposes.

Michael is a World Bank Fellow, author and keynote speaker about leadership, strategy, purpose and international politics. He is the founder of the Kouly Institute and the creator of unique Executive Leadership Programs, that have been delivered to thousands of top business executives, NGO's and government leaders worldwide.

He also dedicates time to various non-profit organizations such as the Middle East Leadership Academy (MELA), Central Eurasia Leadership Academy (CELA), South East Asia Leadership Academy (SEALA) and Leaders Across Boarders (LAB).

His calling is to help people, organizations and countries lead purpose driven lives.

Michael studied at Harvard and Princeton Universities, and is an advisor to state leaders.

Other Books By The Author

BOOK 1 OF THE
SELF-LEADERSHIP BOOK SERIES

FINDING YOUR HUMMUS

This book will provide you, your colleagues, family and friends with insights about life and business to unleash your personal and organizational power.

- Shift happens in life and business, are you ready?

- What is the prime philosophy behind starting a business of growth and sustainable success?

- Do you, your people and business have a guiding purpose? This book is about finding your calling.

- Do you have a personal and organizational strategy to fulfill your purpose? This book is about self awareness, self motivation and self leadership that together can achieve self fulfillment.

- How do you deal with competition, conflict and confusion? This book is rich with empowering inspirational quotes that generate strength and lead to self actualization.

- What is the mindset to lead a life of resilience, abundance and significance? This book is about finding your passion and discovering your way of living a purpose driven life.

BOOK 2 OF THE
SELF-LEADERSHIP BOOK SERIES

If I didn't
Give A ....
I would...

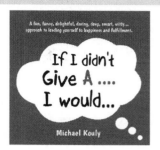

As you will discover, this entertaining book of insightful and witty humor is not like other self leadership books.

WHILE ENJOYING THE EXPERIENCE OF THIS BOOK, YOU'LL ALSO:

- **Blow off steam:** We all have personal issues, challenges, and obstacles that accumulate stress that must be released to keep us in a state of peak motivation.

- **Know yourself:** Sometimes an entire life is spent being stuck at the expense of personal, business, social and relational opportunities for success. Self-discovery is the first step to the healing, actualization, and optimization of your life.

- **Reflect:** Recognizing your priorities, what you really want and what matters most to you is the key to your growth in all aspects of your life.

- **Decide:** To solve problems and catch opportunities, decisions are needed. This book will help you decide and act to expand your potential in a fun, playful, smart and effective way.

- **Lead:** True leadership starts with the self where smart and effective strategy, action and execution are the keys to the growth of our capacity.

BOOK 3 OF THE
SELF-LEADERSHIP BOOK SERIES

MUTE

It doesn't matter who you are or what you do. You carry voices in your head, voices that are always talking to you. Some of the voices whisper, others shout. Some make logical arguments, others create dramas.

Do you know the voices in your head? Do you know where they've come from and how they are controlling you?

As soon as you meet a person, you begin to carry their voice with you. This starts with your parents, loved ones, hated ones, bosses, spouses, heroes, and everyone who is or was significant in your life.

What do these voices want? They want you to live life their way.

What about your freedom? Well, this book is about exactly that: exercising your freedom.

We will look at how you can willingly listen to the encouraging voices and mute the negative ones.

We want to give you the tools to live a happy, successful and fulfilling life that is aligned with your personal purpose and best self.

Life is a blink. There is no time to waste living under the influence of negative voices. Read this book, share it with others, and learn how to lead a life of freedom and meaning so you can become a beautiful voice in the heads of those around you.

WIDE OPEN

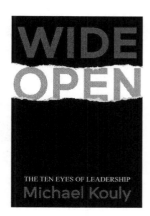

Leadership is a dangerous enterprise, but the rewards are valuable. This book is designed to be your companion in your thrilling journey of remarkable survival and outstanding growth.

THE TEN EYES OF LEADERSHIP
Michael Kouly

THIS UNIQUE AND ILLUMINATING BOOK WILL OPEN YOUR EYES WIDE, SO YOU LEARN MORE ABOUT:

- **Authority:** You are surrounded by authority figures such as parents, bosses, CEOs, presidents, or governments. As you already know, not understanding how to deal with authority is risky.

- **Enemies:** Enemies are a fact of life. They could be passive or aggressive. Enemies want to undermine you and your acts of leadership. Not understanding how to deal with enemies is dangerous.

- **Understanding Yourself and Others:** It is hard to survive and grow and to lead yourself without understanding what drives your thoughts, feelings, words, actions, behaviors, dreams, and ambitions. It is impossible to lead others without understanding them first.

- **Understanding Systems:** We live and work in systems. A system can be a family, team, company, community, city, country or the world. Systems have their unique psychology and rules. Not understanding systems will put your existence and progress at risk, as you may be excluded or isolated from the group that you belong to.

HOW TO
TRUMP THE ENEMY

Some people love you and some don't. When you exercise leadership, some will support you and others will resist, oppose, obstruct, sabotage, or obsessively fight you until you lose.

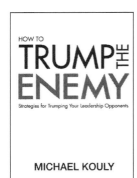

Most attempts at leadership fail not because of how allies are utilized, but because many leaders lack the vital skills necessary for dealing with adversaries.

What will determine your leadership success is mainly your ability to handle those who stand against you.

THIS BOOK IS A UNIQUE AND COMPREHENSIVE REFERENCE THAT YOU CAN CONSULT EVERY TIME YOU DEAL WITH RESISTERS, OPPONENTS, OR ENEMIES.

YOU WILL LEARN MORE ABOUT:

- **Strategies:** There are 104 strategies that you can use separately or in combinations as per the specific nature of the resistance that you are facing.

- **Scenarios:** There are 36 separate scenarios covering seven types of personal, social, organizational, business, and political opponents.

- **Intensities:** There are six intensities of opposition that start from passive and escalate to passive-aggressive, active, active-aggressive, malevolent, and finally archenemy.

- **You:** There is a chapter on YOU acting as your own enemy by allowing your dysfunctional mindsets, beliefs, and habits to sabotage your growth and prevent you from being all that you can be.

BEYOND
STRATEGY

WHY "BEYOND STRATEGY"?

Many people find strategy intimidating, complex, or abstract, but it doesn't have to be.

This book presents a new way of thinking about strategy that is uniquely based upon the Purpose-Driven Growth Model (PDG), in which your organization's purpose and profitability is key to guiding its growth.

- It explores strategy concisely and thoughtfully, examining what the concept encompasses and how strategies can be constructed in a fast-changing and uncertain world.

- It illustrates the differences between strategies that flourish and strategies that languish, and delves into the reasons driving each outcome.

- It offers comprehensive thinking, and tools which view strategy holistically, emphasizing how to lead organizations towards sustainable growth and exceptional performance.

The PDG Model sketches out a practical hybrid of strategy and leadership, that must be unified to fulfill organizational purpose, create growth, and deliver profits. Leadership without strategy is futile, and strategy without leadership is doomed. The two must synchronize to produce results.

Coming Soon

New Titles

by Michael Kouly

THIS IS Leadership

Made in the USA
San Bernardino, CA
15 February 2020